QUOTE OF THE DAY
Inspirational Quotes from Famous People

AARON BARTLETT

QUOTE OF THE DAY
Copyright © 2015 Toppings Publishing
All rights reserved.

Disclaimer
This book is licensed for your personal enjoyment only. This book may not be re-sold or given away to other people. If you would like to share this book with another person, please purchase an additional copy for each recipient. Thank you for respecting the hard work of this author.

Copyright Notes
No part of this publication may be used or reproduced in any form or by any means, including printing, photocopying, or otherwise, without written permission from the author, except in the case of brief quotations embodied in critical articles or review.

If you would like to use material from the book (other than just simply for reviewing the book), prior permission must be obtained by contacting the author at:
aaron.bartlett@toppingspublishing.com.

INTRODUCTION

> Kind words heal and help; cutting words wound and maim.
>
> Proverbs 15:4

The right words at the right time can have a powerful, positive impact on people's lives. When counseling people, I have shared quotes with them to brighten their day and form a positive outlook on life. A few powerful words can inspire people, motivate them, and help them leave old habits behind.

Why are quotes so encouraging to us? In the swirl of activity in everyday life, a quote is the distilled wisdom of a lifetime's worth of experience. Everyone learns something different from the same quote because we bring unique life experiences when we read it. Each quote becomes personalized for us. They speak to where we are and guide us to where we want to be.

In this book are four different quotes for each day that have helped me analyze my life and start each day with a smile. They have helped me and they will help you as well. The quotes will develop insight, ignite creativity, focus your attention, and provide inspiration.

These words will help heal your soul and help you realize your full potential.

> Thanks for reading with me!
> Aaron Bartlett

JANUARY 1

After twelve years of therapy my psychiatrist said something that brought tears to my eyes. He said, 'No hablo ingles.'

Ronnie Shakes

The significant problems we have cannot be solved at the same level of thinking with which we created them.

Albert Einstein (1879 - 1955)
(attributed)

I like to think that I'm a patient, tolerant, woman and that there was no line you could ever cross that would make me stop loving you. But last night you didn't just cross that line, you threw up on it!

Marge Simpson

You talk to God, you're religious. God talks to you, you're psychotic.

Doris Egan, House M.D.
House vs. God, 2006

JANUARY 2

The more you read and observe about this Politics thing, you got to admit that each party is worse than the other. The one that's out always looks the best.

> Will Rogers (1879 - 1935)

Children are all foreigners.

> Ralph Waldo Emerson
> (1803 - 1882)

I believe in equality for everyone, except reporters and photographers.

> Mahatma Gandhi (1869 - 1948)

When I am abroad, I always make it a rule never to criticize or attack the government of my own country. I make up for lost time when I come home.

> Sir Winston Churchill
> (1874 - 1965)

JANUARY 3

Too bad the only people who know how to run the country are busy driving cabs and cutting hair.

> George Burns (1896 - 1996)

Never let your sense of morals get in the way of doing what's right.

> Isaac Asimov (1920 - 1992)

You've got to take the bitter with the sour.

> Samuel Goldwyn (1882 - 1974)

As a matter of principle, I never attend the first annual anything.

> George Carlin (1937 - 2008)

JANUARY 4

Okay, okay, don't panic, whosever problem this is, I'm sure they know how to handle it...Aah! It's my problem! We're doomed!

                        Homer Simpson

Cynics regarded everybody as equally corrupt... Idealists regarded everybody as equally corrupt, except themselves.

                        Robert Anton Wilson

Life isn't fair. It's just fairer than death, that's all.

                        William Goldman

You see things; and you say, 'Why?' But I dream things that never were; and I say, "Why not?"

                        George Bernard Shaw
                             (1856 - 1950)

JANUARY 5

A celebrity is a person who works hard all his life to become well known, then wears dark glasses to avoid being recognized.

> Fred Allen (1894 - 1956)

If you make people think they're thinking, they'll love you; But if you really make them think, they'll hate you.

> Don Marquis (1878 - 1937)

Boyhood, like measles, is one of those complaints which a man should catch young and have done with, for when it comes in middle life it is apt to be serious.

> P. G. Wodehouse
> (1881 - 1975)

Great part of being a grownup, you never have to do anything.

> Peter Blake

JANUARY 6

If computers get too powerful, we can organize them into a committee -- that will do them in.

> Bradley's Bromide

Red meat is NOT bad for you. Now blue-green meat, THAT'S bad for you!

> Tommy Smothers

Honesty is the best policy - when there is money in it.

> Mark Twain (1835 - 1910)

The greatest mystery is not that we have been flung at random between the profusion of matter and of the stars, but that within this prison we can draw from ourselves images powerful enough to deny our nothingness.

> Andre Malraux (1901 - 1976)

JANUARY 7

My Karma ran over your dogma.

> Unknown

It doesn't make a difference what temperature a room is, it's always room temperature.

> Steven Wright (1955 -)

When I'm working on a problem, I never think about beauty. I think only how to solve the problem. But when I have finished, if the solution is not beautiful, I know it is wrong.

> R. Buckminster Fuller
> (1895 - 1983)

A sympathetic Scot summed it all up very neatly in the remark, "You should make a point of trying every experience once, excepting incest and folk dancing."

> Sir Arnold Bax (1883 - 1953)

JANUARY 8

I can't understand it. I can't even understand the people who can understand it.

> Queen Juliana (1909 - 2004)

A lot of people mistake a short memory for a clear conscience.

> Doug Larson

It is hard to believe that a man is telling the truth when you know that you would lie if you were in his place.

> H. L. Mencken (1880 - 1956)

If men could only know each other, they would neither idolize nor hate.

> Elbert Hubbard (1856 - 1915)

JANUARY 9

There's a fine line between genius and insanity. I have erased this line.

> Oscar Levant (1906 - 1972)

Good judgment comes from experience, and experience comes from bad judgment.

> Barry LePatner

The average person thinks he isn't.

> Father Larry Lorenzoni

What happens when the future has come and gone?

> Robert Half

JANUARY 10

I don't really trust a sane person.
> Lyle Alzado (1949 - 1992)

Start every day off with a smile and get it over with.
> W. C. Fields (1880 - 1946)

Oh boy, it looks like it's suicide again for me.
> Moe Szyslak

Some are born great, some achieve greatness, and some hire public relations officers.
> Daniel J. Boorstin (1914 -)

JANUARY 11

Things are only impossible until they're not.

>Hannah Louise Shearer

Before I met my husband, I'd never fallen in love, though I'd stepped in it a few times.

>Rita Rudner

America believes in education: the average professor earns more money in a year than a professional athlete earns in a whole week.

>Evan Esar (1899 - 1995)

There is nothing more dreadful than imagination without taste.

>Johann Wolfgang von Goethe
>(1749 - 1832)

JANUARY 12

In the fight between you and the world, back the world.

> Frank Zappa (1940 - 1993)

The one function TV news performs very well is that when there is no news we give it to you with the same emphasis as if there were.

> David Brinkley (1920 - 2003)

All human situations have their inconveniences. We feel those of the present but neither see nor feel those of the future; and hence we often make troublesome changes without amendment, and frequently for the worse.

> Benjamin Franklin
> (1706 - 1790)

Only exceptionally rational men can afford to be absurd.

> Allan Goldfein

JANUARY 13

It is amazing what you can accomplish if you do not care who gets the credit.

> Harry S. Truman (1884 - 1972)

We don't see things as they are, we see things as we are.

> Anais Nin (1903 - 1977)

What's a soup kitchen?

> Paris Hilton

To punish me for my contempt for authority, fate made me an authority myself.

> Albert Einstein (1879 - 1955)

JANUARY 14

Oh, Marge, cartoons don't have any deep meaning. They're just stupid drawings that give you a cheap laugh.

> Homer Simpson

The man who says he is willing to meet you halfway is usually a poor judge of distance.

> Laurence J. Peter (1919 - 1988)

He hoped and prayed that there wasn't an afterlife. Then he realized there was a contradiction involved here and merely hoped that there wasn't an afterlife.

> Douglas Adams (1952 - 2001)

People might not get all they work for in this world, but they must certainly work for all they get.

> Frederick Douglass
> (1817 - 1895)

JANUARY 15

I have been thinking that I would make a proposition to my Republican friends... that if they will stop telling lies about the Democrats, we will stop telling the truth about them.

> Adlai E. Stevenson Jr.
> (1900 - 1965)

The shortest distance between two points is under construction.

> Noelie Altito

Skeptical scrutiny is the means, in both science and religion, by which deep insights can be winnowed from deep nonsense.

> Carl Sagan (1934 - 1996)

All human beings should try to learn before they die what they are running from, and to, and why.

> James Thurber (1894 - 1961)

JANUARY 16

A specification that will not fit on one page of 8.5x11 inch paper cannot be understood.

> Mark Ardis

The law, in its majestic equality, forbids the rich as well as the poor to sleep under bridges, to beg in the streets, and to steal bread.

> Anatole France (1844 - 1924)

Oh, kids are great! You can teach them to hate what you hate!

> Homer Simpson

Some people have so much respect for their superiors they have none left for themselves.

> Peter McArthur

JANUARY 17

My idea of an agreeable person is a person who agrees with me.

> Benjamin Disraeli (1804 - 1881)

Most people have seen worse things in private than they pretend to be shocked at in public.

> Edgar Watson Howe
> (1853 - 1937)

We are none of us infallible--not even the youngest of us.

> W. H. Thompson

Computer dating is fine, if you're a computer.

> Rita Mae Brown

JANUARY 18

As long as people will accept crap, it will be financially profitable to dispense it.

>Dick Cavett (1936 -)

No man ever listened himself out of a job.

>Calvin Coolidge (1872 - 1933)

Science. What's science ever done for us? TV off.

>Moe Szyslak

Silly things do cease to be silly if they are done by sensible people in an impudent way.

>Jane Austen (1775 - 1817)

JANUARY 19

...when you have eliminated the impossible, whatever remains, however improbable, must be the truth.

> Sir Arthur Conan Doyle
> (1859 - 1930)

A sense of humor is part of the art of leadership, of getting along with people, of getting things done.

> Dwight D. Eisenhower
> (1890 - 1969)

People often write me and ask how I keep my wood floors so clean when I live with a child and a dog, and my answer is that I use a technique called Suffering From a Mental Illness.

> Heather Armstrong

Television – a medium. So called because it is neither rare nor well done.

> Ernie Kovacs

JANUARY 20

Journalism largely consists of saying 'Lord Jones is Dead' to people who never knew that Lord Jones was alive.

> G. K. Chesterton (1874 - 1936)

A rumor without a leg to stand on will get around some other way.

> John Tudor

Nothing shocks me. I'm a scientist.

> Harrison Ford (1942 -)

Never tell anyone that you're writing a book, going on a diet, exercising, taking a course, or quitting smoking. They'll encourage you to death.

> Lynn Johnston (1947 -)

JANUARY 21

Addresses are given to us to conceal our whereabouts.

                        Saki (1870 - 1916)

Now and then an innocent man is sent to the legislature.

               Kin Hubbard (1868 - 1930)

I think that somehow, we learn who we really are and then live with that decision.

            Eleanor Roosevelt (1884 - 1962)

Conscience is what makes a boy tell his mother before his sister does.

                 Evan Esar (1899 - 1995)

JANUARY 22

Seriousness is the only refuge of the shallow.

> Oscar Wilde (1854 - 1900)

Machines take me by surprise with great frequency.

> Alan Turing (1912 - 1954)

Language is the source of misunderstandings.

> Antoine de Saint-Exupery
> (1900 - 1944)

A nuclear reactor is a lot like a woman. You just have to read the manual and press the right buttons.

> Homer Simpson

JANUARY 23

We think in generalities, but we live in detail.

> Alfred North Whitehead
> (1861 - 1947)

No one means all he says, and yet very few say all they mean, for words are slippery and thought is viscous.

> Henry Adams (1838 - 1918)

There are sadistic scientists who hurry to hunt down errors instead of establishing the truth.

> Marie Curie (1867 - 1934)

Being a woman is a terribly difficult task since it consists principally in dealing with men.

> Joseph Conrad (1857 - 1924)

JANUARY 24

You can observe a lot just by watching.

> Yogi Berra (1925 -)

Men are not against you; they are merely for themselves.

> Gene Fowler

The actual tragedies of life bear no relation to one's preconceived ideas. In the event, one is always bewildered by their simplicity, their grandeur of design, and by that element of the bizzare which seems inherent in them.

> Jean Cocteau (1889 - 1963)

The very substance of the ambitious is merely the shadow of a dream.

> William Shakespeare
> (1564 - 1616)

JANUARY 25

I have left orders to be awakened at any time in case of national emergency, even if I'm in a cabinet meeting.

> Ronald Reagan (1911 - 2004)

I believe that professional wrestling is clean and everything else in the world is fixed.

> Frank Deford

Nothing is as simple as we hope it will be.

> Jim Horning

I never teach my pupils. I only attempt to provide the conditions in which they can learn.

> Albert Einstein (1879 - 1955)

JANUARY 26

It is difficult to produce a television documentary that is both incisive and probing when every twelve minutes one is interrupted by twelve dancing rabbits singing about toilet paper.

> Rod Serling (1924 - 1975)

Homer, you're as dumb as a mule and twice as ugly. If a strange man offers you a ride, I say take it!

> Abraham Simpson

All movements go too far.
> Bertrand Russell (1872 - 1970)

She got her looks from her father. He's a plastic surgeon.

> Groucho Marx (1890 - 1977)

JANUARY 27

The gods too are fond of a joke.

> Aristotle (384 BC - 322 BC)

To err is dysfunctional, to forgive co-dependent.

> Berton Averre

Study without desire spoils the memory, and it retains nothing that it takes in.

> Leonardo da Vinci
> (1452 - 1519)

The test for whether or not you can hold a job should not be the arrangement of your chromosomes.

> Bella Abzug (1920 -)

JANUARY 28

When it is not necessary to make a decision, it is necessary not to make a decision.

> Lord Falkland (1610 - 1643)

Half of the modern drugs could well be thrown out of the window, except that the birds might eat them.

> Dr. Martin Henry Fischer

For every action there is an equal and opposite government program.

> Bob Wells

No one really listens to anyone else, and if you try it for a while you'll see why.

> Mignon McLaughlin

JANUARY 29

Every crowd has a silver lining.

> Phineas Taylor Barnum
> (1810 - 1891)

Furious activity is no substitute for understanding.

> H. H. Williams

Try to learn something about everything and everything about something.

> Thomas H. Huxley
> (1825 - 1895)

Ever heard Victoria's REAL secret? Too much support hurts.

> R. Stevens

JANUARY 30

Honesty is a good thing, but it is not profitable to its possessor unless it is kept under control.

> Don Marquis (1878 - 1937)

Facts are stubborn things, but statistics are more pliable.

> Mark Twain (1835 - 1910)

The only time people dislike gossip is when you gossip about them.

> Will Rogers (1879 - 1935)

Nothing like a lot of exercise to make you realize you'd rather be lazy and dead sooner.

> Randy K. Milholland

JANUARY 31

Don't tell people to act their age. It's like telling a baby to move out, and if they're older you're telling them to "die in a hole."

> Devin J. Monroe (1983 -)

Health food makes me sick.

> Calvin Trillin (1935 -)

Most new books are forgotten within a year, especially by those who borrow them.

> Evan Esar (1899 - 1995)

Just in terms of allocation of time resources, religion is not very efficient. There's a lot more I could be doing on a Sunday morning.

> Bill Gates (1955 -)

FEBRUARY 1

You cannot make a man by standing a sheep on its hind legs. But by standing a flock of sheep in that position you can make a crowd of men.

>Max Beerbohm (1872 - 1956)

If men were angels, no government would be necessary.

>James Madison (1751 - 1836)

Wine makes a man more pleased with himself; I do not say that it makes him more pleasing to others.

>Samuel Johnson (1709 - 1784)

Only two things are infinite, the universe and human stupidity, and I'm not sure about the former.

>Albert Einstein (1879 - 1955)

FEBRUARY 2

Ladies and gentlemen, what you are seeing is a total disregard for the things St. Patrick's Day stand for. All this drinking, violence, destruction of property. Are these the things we think of when we think of the Irish?

> Kent Brockman

I'm not a vegetarian because I love animals. I'm a vegetarian because I hate plants.

> A. Whitney Brown

Censorship, like charity, should begin at home; but, unlike charity, it should end there.

> Clare Booth Luce (1903 - 1987)

Humor is by far the most significant activity of the human brain.

> Edward De Bono

FEBRUARY 3

MTV is the lava lamp of the 1980's.

> Doug Ferrari

If your parents never had children, chances are you won't, either.

> Dick Cavett (1936 -)

People demand freedom of speech as a compensation for the freedom of thought which they seldom use.

> Soren Kierkegaard (1813 - 1855)

The reason why so few good books are written is that so few people who can write know anything.

> Walter Bagehot (1826 - 1877)

FEBRUARY 4

Any reviewer who expresses rage and loathing for a novel is preposterous. He or she is like a person who has put on full armor and attacked a hot fudge sundae.

> Kurt Vonnegut (1922 - 2007)

I know that there are people who do not love their fellow man, and I hate people like that!

> Tom Lehrer (1928 -)

One of the keys to happiness is a bad memory.

> Rita Mae Brown

Today's public figures can no longer write their own speeches or books, and there is some evidence that they can't read them either.

> Gore Vidal (1925 -)

FEBRUARY 5

The test of a first-rate intelligence is the ability to hold two opposed ideas in the mind at the same time, and still retain the ability to function.

>F. Scott Fitzgerald (1896 - 1940)

People of Earth! We come to you in the spirit of hostility and menace!

>Kang and Kodos

Two roads diverged in a wood, and I-- I took the one less traveled by, And that has made all the difference.

>Robert Frost (1874 - 1963)

One should as a rule respect public opinion in so far as is necessary to avoid starvation and to keep out of prison, but anything that goes beyond this is voluntary submission to an unnecessary tyranny, and is likely to interfere with happiness in all kinds of ways.

>Bertrand Russell (1872 - 1970)

FEBRUARY 6

Life is divided into the horrible and the miserable.

> Woody Allen (1935 -)

Blessed is the man who, having nothing to say, abstains from giving wordy evidence of the fact.

> George Eliot (1819 - 1880)

My Grandmother is over eighty and still doesn't need glasses. Drinks right out of the bottle.

> Henny Youngman (1906 - 1998)

Anybody who has doubts about the ingenuity or the resourcefulness of a plumber never got a bill from one.

> George Meany

FEBRUARY 7

Yesterday I was a dog. Today I'm a dog. Tomorrow I'll probably still be a dog. Sigh! There's so little hope for advancement.

> Charles M. Schulz (1922 - 2000)

Neurotics build castles in the air, psychotics live in them. My mother cleans them.

> Rita Rudner

Ok Marge, we can go to the circus. Maybe I can finally find out why a man would think a stool is a proper defense against a lion.

> Homer Simpson

I shall not waste my days in trying to prolong them.

> Ian Fleming (1908 - 1964)

FEBRUARY 8

Every nation ridicules other nations, and all are right.

   Arthur Schopenhauer (1788 - 1860)

That you may retain your self-respect, it is better to displease the people by doing what you know is right, than to temporarily please them by doing what you know is wrong.

                    William J. H. Boetcker

It's a dangerous business going out your front door.

                  J. R. R. Tolkien (1892 - 1973)

Sometimes the mind, for reasons we don't necessarily understand, just decides to go to the store for a quart of milk.

                      Diane Frolov and
                    Andrew Schneider

FEBRUARY 9

Clothes make the man. Naked people have little or no influence on society.

> Mark Twain (1835 - 1910)

He has all the virtues I dislike and none of the vices I admire.

> Sir Winston Churchill
> (1874 - 1965)

Ninety percent of the politicians give the other ten percent a bad reputation.

> Henry Kissinger (1923 -)

Whenever you want to talk to me, just call me on the phone and tell me to turn on my walkie-talkie.

> Bart Simpson

FEBRUARY 10

The cloning of humans is on most of the lists of things to worry about from Science, along with behaviour control, genetic engineering, transplanted heads, computer poetry and the unrestrained growth of plastic flowers.

Lewis Thomas (1913 - 1993)

The most important kind of freedom is to be what you really are. You trade in your reality for a role. You give up your ability to feel, and in exchange, put on a mask.

Jim Morrison (1943 - 1971)

I'd be mortified if someone ever made a lousy product with the Simpson name on it.

Lisa Simpson

We Americans live in a nation where the medical-care system is second to none in the world, unless you count maybe 25 or 30 little scuzzball countries like Scotland that we could vaporize in seconds if we felt like it.

Dave Barry (1947 -)

FEBRUARY 11

There are three kinds of lies: lies, damned lies, and statistics.

> Benjamin Disraeli (1804 - 1881)

Fortune can, for her pleasure, fools advance, And toss them on the wheels of Chance.

> Juvenal (55 AD - 127 AD)

I feel about airplanes the way I feel about diets. It seems to me they are wonderful things for other people to go on.

> Jean Kerr

In the end, we will remember not the words of our enemies, but the silence of our friends.

> Martin Luther King Jr.
> (1929 - 1968)

FEBRUARY 12

After an access cover has been secured by 16 hold-down screws, it will be discovered that the gasket has been omitted.

> De la Lastra's Corollary

People with courage and character always seem sinister to the rest.

> Hermann Hesse (1877 - 1962)

Would those of you in the cheaper seats clap your hands? And the rest of you, if you'll just rattle your jewelry.

> John Lennon (1940 - 1980)

It's hard to take over the world when you sleep 20 hours a day.

> Darby Conley

FEBRUARY 13

You know Marge, getting old is a terrible thing. I think the saddest day of my life was when I realized I could beat my Dad at most things, and Bart experienced that at the age of four.

> Homer Simpson

A person who trusts no one can't be trusted.

> Jerome Blattner

Now I know what a statesman is; he's a dead politician. We need more statesmen.

> Bob Edwards

At least half the mystery novels published violate the law that the solution, once revealed, must seem to be inevitable.

> Raymond Chandler (1888 - 1959)

FEBRUARY 14

I do not fear computers. I fear the lack of them.

>Isaac Asimov (1920 - 1992)

He wrapped himself in quotations- as a beggar would enfold himself in the purple of Emperors.

>Rudyard Kipling (1865 - 1936)

There is not any memory with less satisfaction than the memory of some temptation we resisted.

>James Branch Cabell
>(1879 - 1958)

No man needs a vacation so much as the man who has just had one.

>Elbert Hubbard (1856 - 1915)

FEBRUARY 15

A man thinks that by mouthing hard words he understands hard things.

>Herman Melville (1819 - 1891)

It is inaccurate to say that I hate everything. I am strongly in favor of common sense, common honesty, and common decency. This makes me forever ineligible for public office.

>H. L. Mencken (1880 - 1956)

The incompetent with nothing to do can still make a mess of it.

>Laurence J. Peter (1919 - 1988)

That all men are equal is a proposition which, at ordinary times, no sane individual has ever given his assent.

>Aldous Huxley (1894 - 1963)

FEBRUARY 16

When you come to a fork in the road, take it.

> Yogi Berra (1925 -)

Sure I'm for helping the elderly. I'm going to be old myself some day.

> Lillian Carter

At 18 our convictions are hills from which we look; At 45 they are caves in which we hide.

> F. Scott Fitzgerald (1896 - 1940)

There are two motives for reading a book: one, that you enjoy it; the other, that you can boast about it.

> Bertrand Russell (1872 - 1970)

FEBRUARY 17

How can you govern a country which has 246 varieties of cheese?

> Charles De Gaulle (1890 - 1970)

Hegel was right when he said that we learn from history that man can never learn anything from history.

> George Bernard Shaw
> (1856 - 1950)

I had a monumental idea this morning, but I didn't like it.

> Samuel Goldwyn (1882 - 1974)

A short saying oft contains much wisdom.

> Sophocles (496 BC - 406 BC)

FEBRUARY 18

Although prepared for martyrdom, I preferred that it be postponed.

> Sir Winston Churchill
> (1874 - 1965)

Good teaching is one-fourth preparation and three-fourths theater.

> Gail Godwin

The point of living and of being an optimist, is to be foolish enough to believe the best is yet to come.

> Peter Ustinov (1921 - 2004)

For aught that I could ever read, could ever hear by tale or history, the course of true love never did run smooth.

> William Shakespeare
> (1564 - 1616)

FEBRUARY 19

The marvel of all history is the patience with which men and women submit to burdens unnecessarily laid upon them by their governments.

William H. Borah

Some circumstantial evidence is very strong, as when you find a trout in the milk.

Henry David Thoreau
(1817 - 1862)

There is a great deal of difference between an eager man who wants to read a book and the tired man who wants a book to read.

G. K. Chesterton (1874 - 1936)

A girl phoned me the other day and said "Come on over, there's nobody home." I went over. Nobody was home.

Rodney Dangerfield (1921 - 2004)

FEBRUARY 20

Good-bye. I am leaving because I am bored.

> George Saunders

Correct me if I'm wrong, but hasn't the fine line between sanity and madness gotten finer?

> George Price

Criminal: A person with predatory instincts who has not sufficient capital to form a corporation.

> Howard Scott (1926 -)

When I do good, I feel good; when I do bad, I feel bad, and that is my religion.

> Abraham Lincoln (1809 - 1865)

FEBRUARY 21

An intellectual snob is someone who can listen to the William Tell Overture and not think of The Lone Ranger.

> Dan Rather (1931 -)

The illiterate of the 21st century will not be those who cannot read and write, but those who cannot learn, unlearn, and relearn.

> Alvin Toffler

Normal is getting dressed in clothes that you buy for work and driving through traffic in a car that you are still paying for - in order to get to the job you need to pay for the clothes and the car, and the house you leave vacant all day so you can afford to live in it.

> Ellen Goodman (1941 -)

I never guess. It is a capital mistake to theorize before one has data. Insensibly one begins to twist facts to suit theories, instead of theories to suit facts.

> Sir Arthur Conan Doyle
> (1859 - 1930)

FEBRUARY 22

It's kind of fun to do the impossible.
>Walt Disney (1901 - 1966)

A verbal contract isn't worth the paper it's written on.
>Samuel Goldwyn (1882 - 1974)

I think that one possible definition of our modern culture is that it is one in which nine-tenths of our intellectuals can't read any poetry.
>Randall Jarrell (1914 - 1965)

When the gods wish to punish us, they answer our prayers.
>Oscar Wilde (1854 - 1900)

FEBRUARY 23

No opera plot can be sensible, for people do not sing when they are feeling sensible.

> W. H. Auden (1907 - 1973)

Give a man a fish and he will eat for a day. Teach a man to fish and he will eat for a lifetime. Teach a man to create an artificial shortage of fish and he will eat steak.

> Jay Leno (1950 -)

Nothing travels faster than the speed of light with the possible exception of bad news, which obeys its own special laws.

> Douglas Adams (1952 - 2001)

This is the sixth book I've written, which isn't bad for a guy who's only read two.

> George Burns (1896 - 1996)

FEBRUARY 24

I hope I didn't brain my damage.

> Homer Simpson

Love is the difficult realization that something other than oneself is real.

> Iris Murdoch (1919 - 1999)

Who is more busy than he who hath least to do?

> John Clarke

Nothing can be so amusingly arrogant as a young man who has just discovered an old idea and thinks it is his own.

> Sidney J. Harris

FEBRUARY 25

Some people will never learn anything because they understand everything too soon.

> Alexander Pope (1688 - 1744)

To die for an idea; it is unquestionably noble. But how much nobler it would be if men died for ideas that were true!

> H. L. Mencken (1880 - 1956)

The man who lets himself be bored is even more contemptible than the bore.

> Samuel Butler (1835 - 1902)

Insane people are always sure that they are fine. It is only the sane people who are willing to admit that they are crazy.

> Nora Ephron

FEBRUARY 26

I've had a perfectly wonderful evening. But this wasn't it.

> Groucho Marx (1890 - 1977)

You couldn't even prove the White House staff sane beyond a reasonable doubt.

> Ed Meese (1931 -)

Patience has its limits. Take it too far, and it's cowardice.

> George Jackson (1941 - 1971)

Human Dignity has gleamed only now and then and here and there, in lonely splendor, throughout the ages, a hope of the better men, never an achievement of the majority.

> James Thurber (1894 - 1961)

FEBRUARY 27

I'm not a real movie star. I've still got the same wife I started out with twenty-eight years ago.

> Will Rogers (1879 - 1935)

This paperback is very interesting, but I find it will never replace a hardcover book - it makes a very poor doorstop.

> Alfred Hitchcock (1899 - 1980)

A truly great book should be read in youth, again in maturity and once more in old age, as a fine building should be seen by morning light, at noon and by moonlight.

> Robertson Davies

People want economy and they will pay any price to get it.

> Lee Iacocca (1924 -)

FEBRUARY 28

I work like I drink: alone, or with a monkey watching.

> Krusty the Clown

You can no more win a war than you can win an earthquake.

> Jeannette Rankin (1880 - 1973)

I love Africa in general. South Africa and West Africa, they are both great countries.

> Paris Hilton

He who praises you for what you lack wishes to take from you what you have.

> Don Juan Manuel (1282 - 1349)

MARCH 1

There used to be a real me, but I had it surgically removed.
> Peter Sellers (1925 - 1980)

A censor is a man who knows more than he thinks you ought to.
> Granville Hicks (1901 - 1982)

You can't have everything. Where would you put it?
> Steven Wright (1955 -)

I have lost friends, some by death... others through sheer inability to cross the street.
> Virginia Woolf (1882 - 1941)

MARCH 2

I'm too shy to express my sexual needs except over the phone to people I don't know.

> Garry Shandling (1949 -)

There are three social classes in America: upper middle class, middle class, and lower middle class.

> Judith Martin

I find nothing more depressing than optimism.

> Paul Fussell

The days of the digital watch are numbered.

> Tom Stoppard (1937 -)

MARCH 3

The meek shall inherit the Earth, but not its mineral rights.

> J. Paul Getty (1892 - 1976)

Aristotle was famous for knowing everything. He taught that the brain exists merely to cool the blood and is not involved in the process of thinking. This is true only of certain persons.

> Will Cuppy

People say that life is the thing, but I prefer reading.

> Logan Pearsall Smith
> (1865 - 1946)

Like so many Americans, she was trying to construct a life that made sense from things she found in gift shops.

> Kurt Vonnegut (1922 - 2007)

MARCH 4

Reality is nothing but a collective hunch.

> Jane Wagner

Life is a long lesson in humility.
> James M. Barrie (1860 - 1937)

Some mornings it just doesn't seem worth it to gnaw through the leather straps.

> Emo Phillips

At the age of eleven or thereabouts women acquire a poise and an ability to handle difficult situations which a man, if he is lucky, manages to achieve somewhere in the later seventies.

> P. G. Wodehouse (1881 - 1975)

MARCH 5

If I had to live my life again, I'd make the same mistakes, only sooner.

    Tallulah Bankhead (1903 - 1968)

Where a calculator on the ENIAC is equipped with 18,000 vacuum tubes and weighs 30 tons, computers in the future may have only 1,000 vaccuum tubes and perhaps weigh 1.5 tons.

    Unknown

What we think, or what we know, or what we believe is, in the end, of little consequence. The only consequence is what we do.

    John Ruskin (1819 - 1900)

Oops, lost a nail. Well, that's leprosy for you.

    Montgomery Burns

MARCH 6

Health nuts are going to feel stupid someday, lying in hospitals dying of nothing.

> Redd Foxx (1922 - 1991)

Ordinarily he was insane, but he had lucid moments when he was merely stupid.

> Heinrich Heine (1797 - 1856)

Inanimate objects are classified scientifically into three major categories - those that don't work, those that break down and those that get lost.

> Russell Baker (1925 -)

When the going gets weird, the weird turn pro.

> Hunter S. Thompson
> (1939 - 2005)

MARCH 7

Sometimes I worry about being a success in a mediocre world.

>Lily Tomlin (1939 -)

Nothing changes your opinion of a friend so surely as success - yours or his.

>Franklin P. Jones

Whenever you have an efficient government you have a dictatorship.

>Harry S Truman (1884 - 1972)

Silence propagates itself, and the longer talk has been suspended, the more difficult it is to find anything to say.

>Samuel Johnson (1709 - 1784)

MARCH 8

I belong to no organized party. I am a Democrat.

>Will Rogers (1879 - 1935)

There's a whiff of the lynch mob or the lemming migration about any overlarge concentration of like-thinking individuals, no matter how virtuous their cause.

>P. J. O'Rourke (1947 -)
>Parliament of Whores (1991)

There is absolutely no inevitability as long as there is a willingness to contemplate what is happening.

>Marshall McLuhan (1911 - 1980)

We are all apt to believe what the world believes about us.

>George Eliot (1819 - 1880)

MARCH 9

People who work sitting down get paid more than people who work standing up.

> Ogden Nash (1902 - 1971)

Yes, we have to divide up our time like that, between our politics and our equations. But to me our equations are far more important, for politics are only a matter of present concern. A mathematical equation stands forever.

> Albert Einstein (1879 - 1955)

An adventure is only an inconvenience rightly considered. An inconvenience is an adventure wrongly considered.

> G. K. Chesterton (1874 - 1936)

Stuffed deer heads on walls are bad enough, but it's worse when they are wearing dark glasses and have streamers in their antlers because then you know they were enjoying themselves at a party when they were shot.

> Ellen DeGeneres

MARCH 10

Technology is a way of organizing the universe so that man doesn't have to experience it.

> Max Frisch

I tend to live in the past because most of my life is there.

> Herb Caen

Life is too short for traffic.

> Dan Bellack

What we call 'Progress' is the exchange of one nuisance for another nuisance.

> Havelock Ellis (1859 - 1939)

MARCH 11

Nobody believes the official spokesman... but everybody trusts an unidentified source.

> Ron Nesen

The brain is a wonderful organ. It starts working the moment you get up in the morning and does not stop until you get into the office.

> Robert Frost (1874 - 1963)

But what is the difference between literature and journalism? ...Journalism is unreadable and literature is not read. That is all.

> Oscar Wilde (1854 - 1900)

I'm tired of all this nonsense about beauty being only skin-deep. That's deep enough. What do you want, an adorable pancreas?

> Jean Kerr

MARCH 12

I bought some batteries, but they weren't included.

> Steven Wright (1955 -)

I like work: it fascinates me. I can sit and look at it for hours.

> Jerome K. Jerome (1859 - 1927)

Time sneaks up on you like a windshield on a bug.

> John Lithgow

The trouble with having an open mind, of course, is that people will insist on coming along and trying to put things in it.

> Terry Pratchett

MARCH 13

A coupla months in the laboratory can save a coupla hours in the library.

> Westheimer's Discovery

Human beings are seventy percent water, and with some the rest is collagen.

> Martin Mull (1943 -)

You can never underestimate the stupidity of the general public.

> Scott Adams (1957 -)

Electricity is actually made up of extremely tiny particles called electrons, that you cannot see with the naked eye unless you have been drinking.

> Dave Barry (1947 -)

MARCH 14

To you I'm an atheist; to God, I'm the Loyal Opposition.

                        Woody Allen (1935 -)

Save a little money each month and at the end of the year you'll be surprised at how little you have.

                        Ernest Haskins

A liberal is a person whose interests aren't at stake at the moment.

                        Willis Player

A great many people think they are thinking when they are really rearranging their prejudices.

                        William James (1842 - 1910)

MARCH 15

The author of the Iliad is either Homer or, if not Homer, somebody else of the same name.

> Aldous Huxley (1894 - 1963)

We forfeit three-fourths of ourselves in order to be like other people.

> Arthur Schopenhauer
> (1788 - 1860)

Platitude: an idea (a) that is admitted to be true by everyone, and (b) that is not true.

> H. L. Mencken (1880 - 1956)

What is life but a series of inspired follies? The difficulty is to find them to do. Never lose a chance: it doesn't come every day.

> George Bernard Shaw
> (1856 - 1950)

MARCH 16

O Lord, help me to be pure, but not yet.

>Saint Augustine
>(354 AD - 430 AD)

Isn't it interesting that the same people who laugh at science fiction listen to weather forecasts and economists?

>Kelvin Throop III

If I only had a little humility, I'd be perfect.

>Ted Turner

If fifty million people say a foolish thing, it is still a foolish thing.

>Anatole France (1844 - 1924)

MARCH 17

I dote on his very absence.

> William Shakespeare
> (1564 - 1616)

Man is tormented by no greater anxiety than to find someone quickly to whom he can hand over that great gift of freedom with which the ill-fated creature is born.

> Fyodor Dostoevsky
> (1821 - 1881)

If you can't say anything good about someone, sit right here by me.

> Alice Roosevelt Longworth
> (1884 - 1980)

Men are generally idle, and ready to satisfy themselves, and intimidate the industry of others, by calling that impossible which is only difficult.

> Samuel Johnson (1709 - 1784)

MARCH 18

See what will happen if you don't stop biting your fingernails?

>Will Rogers (1879 - 1935)

There is always some madness in love. But there is also always some reason in madness.

>Friedrich Nietzsche
>(1844 - 1900)

The only way to make a man trustworthy is to trust him.

>Henry Stimson (1867 - 1950)

I have been through some terrible things in my life, some of which actually happened.

>Mark Twain (1835 - 1910)

MARCH 19

Everybody likes a kidder, but nobody lends him money.

>Arthur Miller (1915 - 2005)

I hate women because they always know where things are.

>James Thurber (1894 - 1961)

The problem with people who have no vices is that generally you can be pretty sure they're going to have some pretty annoying virtues.

>Elizabeth Taylor (1932 -)

If you don't know to the second when a drunk's gonna vomit on you, you don't survive as a strip club bouncer.

>Veronica Pare
>and Ferrett Steinmetz

MARCH 20

I like life. It's something to do.
> Ronnie Shakes

You don't win friends with salad.
> Homer Simpson

Expose yourself to your deepest fear; after that, fear has no power, and the fear of freedom shrinks and vanishes. You are free.
> Jim Morrison (1943 - 1971)

The Internet is like alcohol in some sense. It accentuates what you would do anyway. If you want to be a loner, you can be more alone. If you want to connect, it makes it easier to connect.
> Esther Dyson

MARCH 21

Look, I don't care if Ned Flanders is the nicest guy in the world, he's a jerk!

>Homer Simpson

Don't accept rides from strange men, and remember that all men are strange.

>Robin Morgan

I have found the best way to give advice to your children is to find out what they want and then advise them to do it.

>Harry S Truman (1884 - 1972)

I was the kid next door's imaginary friend.

>Emo Phillips

MARCH 22

Committee--a group of men who individually can do nothing but as a group decide that nothing can be done.

> Fred Allen (1894 - 1956)

I disapprove of what you say, but I will defend to the death your right to say it.

> Voltaire (1694 - 1778)

The most wasted of all days is one without laughter.

> e e cummings (1894 - 1962)

I don't have a photograph, but you can have my footprints. They're upstairs in my socks.

> Groucho Marx (1890 - 1977)

MARCH 23

Advertising may be described as the science of arresting the human intelligence long enough to get money from it.

>Stephen Leacock (1869 - 1944)

People will buy anything that is one to a customer.

>Sinclair Lewis (1885 - 1951)

Where humor is concerned there are no standards - no one can say what is good or bad, although you can be sure that everyone will.

>John Kenneth Galbraith
>(1908 - 2006)

My theory is that all of Scottish cuisine is based on a dare.

>Mike Myers

MARCH 24

Our scientific power has outrun our spiritual power. We have guided missiles and misguided men.

> Martin Luther King Jr.
> (1929 - 1968)

The idea of all-out nuclear war is unsettling.

> Walter Goodman

There are more of them than us.

> Herb Caen

Happiness in intelligent people is the rarest thing I know.

> Ernest Hemingway
> (1899 - 1961)

MARCH 25

The louder he talked of his honor, the faster we counted our spoons.

> Ralph Waldo Emerson
> (1803 - 1882)

There's no present. There's only the immediate future and the recent past.

> George Carlin (1937 - 2008)

There are only two kinds of people who are really fascinating: people who know absolutely everything, and people who know absolutely nothing.

> Oscar Wilde (1854 - 1900)

I've accepted that I'm not going to die of natural causes, [but] getting killed 'cuz you're naturally a dick seems like natural causes to me.

> Randy K. Milholland

MARCH 26

As I was walking up the stair
I met a man who wasn't there.
He wasn't there again today.
I wish, I wish he'd stay away.

>Hughes Mearns

I can think of nothing more boring for the American people than to have to sit in their living rooms for a whole half hour looking at my face on their television screens.

>Dwight D. Eisenhower
>(1890 - 1969)

I not only use all the brains that I have, but all that I can borrow.

>Woodrow Wilson (1856 - 1924)

Are cartoons too violent for children? Most people would say "No, of course not, what kind of stupid question is that?" But one woman says "Yes"... Marge Simpson.

>Kent Brockman

MARCH 27

Who would have guessed reading and writing would pay off?

> Homer Simpson

It is a common delusion that you make things better by talking about them.

> Dame Rose Macaulay
> (1881 - 1958)

I find that a great part of the information I have was acquired by looking up something and finding something else on the way.

Franklin P. Adams (1881 - 1960)

Misquotation is, in fact, the pride and privilege of the learned. A widely-read man never quotes accurately, for the rather obvious reason that he has read too widely.

> Hesketh Pearson

MARCH 28

Doing a thing well is often a waste of time.

> Robert Byrne

What is the difference between unethical and ethical advertising? Unethical advertising uses falsehoods to deceive the public; ethical advertising uses truth to deceive the public.

> Vilhjalmur Stefansson
> (1879 - 1962)

The only thing that makes life possible is permanent, intolerable uncertainty; not knowing what comes next.

> Ursula K. LeGuin

The wages of sin are death, but by the time taxes are taken out, it's just sort of a tired feeling.

> Paula Poundstone

MARCH 29

Behind the phony tinsel of Hollywood lies the real tinsel.

> Oscar Levant (1906 - 1972)

You see, wire telegraph is a kind of a very, very long cat. You pull his tail in New York and his head is meowing in Los Angeles. Do you understand this? And radio operates exactly the same way: you send signals here, they receive them there. The only difference is that there is no cat.

> Albert Einstein (1879 - 1955)

Every increased possession loads us with new weariness.

> John Ruskin (1819 - 1900)

Mediocrity knows nothing higher than itself, but talent instantly recognizes genius.

> Sir Arthur Conan Doyle
> (1859 - 1930)

MARCH 30

Nobody outside of a baby carriage or a judge's chamber believes in an unprejudiced point of view.

                Lillian Hellman (1905 - 1984)

Half of the American people have never read a newspaper. Half never voted for President. One hopes it is the same half.

                      Gore Vidal (1925 -)

Where is human nature so weak as in the bookstore?

                    Henry Ward Beecher
                          (1813 - 1887)

Liberty means responsibility. That is why most men dread it.

                    George Bernard Shaw
                          (1856 - 1950)

MARCH 31

Life is full of misery, loneliness, and suffering - and it's all over much too soon.

> Woody Allen (1935 -)

The only paradise is paradise lost.
> Marcel Proust (1871 - 1922)

I have always felt that a politician is to be judged by the animosities he excites among his opponents.

> Sir Winston Churchill
> (1874 - 1965)

Writing gives you the illusion of control, and then you realize it's just an illusion, that people are going to bring their own stuff into it.

> David Sedaris

APRIL 1

Homer, you have to stop dropping your pants for everyone who claims they're a doctor.

> Marge Simpson

The only difference between the Democrats and the Republicans is that the Democrats allow the poor to be corrupt, too.

> Oscar Levant (1906 - 1972)

Where all think alike, no one thinks very much.

> Walter Lippmann (1889 - 1974)

The whole secret of life is to be interested in one thing profoundly and in a thousand things well.

> Horace Walpole (1717 - 1797)

APRIL 2

Of all noises, I think music is the least disagreeable.
> Samuel Johnson (1709 - 1784)

God help those who do not help themselves.
> Wilson Mizner (1876 - 1933)

Politics is the skilled use of blunt objects.
> Lester B. Pearson (1897 - 1972)

It is a wise father that knows his own child.
> William Shakespeare (1564 - 1616)

APRIL 3

My favorite thing about the Internet is that you get to go into the private world of real creeps without having to smell them.

> Penn Jillette (1955 -)

To alcohol! The cause of, and solution to, all of life's problems.

> Homer Simpson

Not every heiress is famous. Or fun. There are a lot of boring heiresses out there.

> Paris Hilton

Dear God, give a bald guy a break. Amen.

> Homer Simpson

APRIL 4

Very little is known of the Canadian country since it is rarely visited by anyone but the Queen and illiterate sport fishermen.

> P. J. O'Rourke (1947 -)

Democracy means that anyone can grow up to be president, and anyone who doesn't grow up can be vice president.

> Johnny Carson (1925 - 2005)

The length of a film should be directly related to the endurance of the human bladder.

> Alfred Hitchcock (1899 - 1980)

The effort to understand the universe is one of the very few things that lifts human life a little above the level of farce, and gives it some of the grace of tragedy.

> Steven Weinberg (1933 -)

APRIL 5

We're not lost. We're locationally challenged.

> John M. Ford

Americans detest all lies except lies spoken in public or printed lies.

> Edgar Watson Howe
> (1853 - 1937)

Absolute faith corrupts as absolutely as absolute power.

> Eric Hoffer (1902 - 1983)

Every generation imagines itself to be more intelligent than the one that went before it, and wiser than the one that comes after it.

> George Orwell (1903 - 1950)

APRIL 6

I am a kind of paranoiac in reverse. I suspect people of plotting to make me happy.

>J. D. Salinger (1919 -)

Everyone wants to be Cary Grant. Even I want to be Cary Grant.

>Cary Grant (1904 - 1986)

Television is for appearing on - not for looking at.

>Noel Coward (1899 - 1973)

If the fans don't wanna come out to the ballpark, no one can stop 'em.

>Yogi Berra (1925 -)

APRIL 7

So a few people won't get a few letters, boo hoo! You know the kind of letters people write. Dear somebody you never heard of, how was so and so, blah blah blah blah blah blah blah, yours truly, some bozo, big loss!

> Homer Simpson

Consistency is the last refuge of the unimaginative.

> Oscar Wilde (1854 - 1900)

A prose writer gets tired of writing prose, and wants to be a poet. So he begins every line with a capital letter, and keeps on writing prose.

> Samuel McChord Crothers

The nice part about being a pessimist is that you are constantly being either proven right or pleasantly surprised.

> George F. Will (1941 -)

APRIL 8

To succeed in the world it is not enough to be stupid, you must also be well-mannered.

> Voltaire (1694 - 1778)

Some people are born on third base and go through life thinking they hit a triple.

> Barry Switzer (1937 -)

I am not a scalper, I'm just a dude whose 200 friends did not show up.

> Simpsons Ticket Scalper

If a dog jumps in your lap, it is because he is fond of you; but if a cat does the same thing, it is because your lap is warmer.

> Alfred North Whitehead
> (1861 - 1947)

APRIL 9

Why is this thus? What is the reason for this thusness?

> Artemus Ward (1834 - 1867)

Parents were invented to make children happy by giving them something to ignore.

> Ogden Nash (1902 - 1971)

Everything in the world may be endured except continued prosperity.

> Johann Wolfgang von Goethe
> (1749 - 1832)

We have so much time and so little to do. Strike that, reverse it.

> Roald Dahl (1916 - 1990)

APRIL 10

Aristotle maintained that women have fewer teeth than men; although he was twice married, it never occurred to him to verify this statement by examining his wives' mouths.

            Bertrand Russell (1872 - 1970)

He can compress the most words into the smallest ideas of any man I ever met.

            Abraham Lincoln (1809 - 1865)

You failed, Seymour. What is it with you and failure?

            Agnes Skinner

I am against using death as a punishment. I am also against using it as a reward.

            Stanislaw J. Lec (1909 - 1966)

APRIL 11

I believe we are on an irreversible trend toward more freedom and democracy - but that could change.

> Dan Quayle (1947 -)

Beware of the man who works hard to learn something, learns it, and finds himself no wiser than before... He is full of murderous resentment of people who are ignorant without having come by their ignorance the hard way.

> Kurt Vonnegut (1922 - 2007)

No one has ever had an idea in a dress suit.

> Sir Frederick G. Banting
> (1891 - 1941)

You can live to be a hundred if you give up all the things that make you want to live to be a hundred.

> Woody Allen (1935 -)

APRIL 12

I can't understand why people are frightened of new ideas. I'm frightened of the old ones.

>John Cage (1912 - 1992)

I finally figured out the only reason to be alive is to enjoy it.

>Rita Mae Brown

I don't like composers who think. It gets in the way of their plagiarism.

>Howard Dietz

Look for the ridiculous in everything and you will find it.

>Jules Renard (1864 - 1910)

APRIL 13

It is always the best policy to speak the truth--unless, of course, you are an exceptionally good liar.

Jerome K. Jerome
(1859 - 1927)

I'd rather let a thousand guilty men go free than chase after them.

Clancy Wiggum

You cannot shake hands with a clenched fist.

Indira Gandhi (1917 - 1984)

The two symbols of the Republican Party: an elephant, and a big fat white guy who is threatened by change.

Seth MacFarlane

APRIL 14

Inspiration is wonderful when it happens, but the writer must develop an approach for the rest of the time... The wait is simply too long.

> Leonard Bernstein
> (1918 - 1990)

Always be nice to your children because they are the ones who will choose your rest home.

> Phyllis Diller

Free advice is worth the price.

> Robert Half

In preparing for this debate, I did a little research, and I discovered something astonishing. There was violence in the past, long before cartoons were invented.

> Roger Meyers Jr.

APRIL 15

It's not easy to juggle a pregnant wife and a troubled child, but somehow I managed to fit in eight hours of TV a day.

      Homer Simpson

Do I contradict myself? Very well then I contradict myself, (I am large, I contain multitudes.)

     Walt Whitman (1819 - 1892)

Rage is the only quality which has kept me, or anybody I have ever studied, writing columns for newspapers.

      Jimmy Breslin

In the beginning there was nothing. God said, 'Let there be light!' And there was light. There was still nothing, but you could see it a whole lot better.

      Ellen DeGeneres

APRIL 16

If one sticks too rigidly to one's principles, one would hardly see anybody.

> Agatha Christie (1890 - 1976)

If the world should blow itself up, the last audible voice would be that of an expert saying it can't be done.

> Peter Ustinov (1921 - 2004)

Eccentricity is not, as dull people would have us believe, a form of madness. It is often a kind of innocent pride, and the man of genius and the aristocrat are frequently regarded as eccentrics because genius and aristocrat are entirely unafraid of and uninfluenced by the opinions and vagaries of the crowd.

> Edith Sitwell (1887 - 1964)

Computer games don't affect kids, I mean if Pac Man affected us as kids, we'd all be running around in darkened rooms, munching pills and listening to repetitive music.

> Marcus Brigstocke

APRIL 17

Imagine if every Thursday your shoes exploded if you tied them the usual way. This happens to us all the time with computers, and nobody thinks of complaining.

> Jef Raskin

Drinking makes such fools of people, and people are such fools to begin with, that it's compounding a felony.

> Robert Benchley (1889 - 1945)

Everything that irritates us about others can lead us to an understanding of ourselves.

> Carl Jung (1875 - 1961)

Barring that natural expression of villainy which we all have, the man looked honest enough.

> Mark Twain (1835 - 1910)

APRIL 18

Puritanism: The haunting fear that someone, somewhere, may be happy.

>H. L. Mencken (1880 - 1956)

I bought a cactus. A week later it died. And I got depressed, because I thought, Damn. I am less nurturing than a desert.

>Demetri Martin

A husband is like a fire, he goes out when unattended.

>Evan Esar (1899 - 1995)

That's what college is for - getting as many bad decisions as possible out of the way before you're forced into the real world. I keep a checklist of 'em on the wall in my room.

>Jeph Jacques

APRIL 19

A superstition is a premature explanation that overstays its time.

> George Iles

Reading this book is like waiting for the first shoe to drop.

> Ralph Novak

A healthy male adult bore consumes each year one and a half times his own weight in other people's patience.

> John Updike (1932 -)

Nothing in life is to be feared, it is only to be understood. Now is the time to understand more, so that we may fear less.

> Marie Curie (1867 - 1934)

APRIL 20

It is dangerous to be right when the government is wrong.

> Voltaire (1694 - 1778)

Men have become the tools of their tools.

> Henry David Thoreau
> (1817 - 1862)

The only thing I was fit for was to be a writer, and this notion rested solely on my suspicion that I would never be fit for real work, and that writing didn't require any.

> Russell Baker (1925 -)

Adventure is just bad planning.

> Roald Amundsen (1872 - 1928)

APRIL 21

There is no human problem which could not be solved if people would simply do as I advise.

Gore Vidal (1925 -)

Liberals are very broadminded: they are always willing to give careful consideration to both sides of the same side.

Anonymous

Sometimes I think the surest sign that intelligent life exists elsewhere in the universe is that none of it has tried to contact us.

Bill Watterson (1958 -)

The whole dream of democracy is to raise the proletarian to the level of stupidity attained by the bourgeois.

Gustave Flaubert
(1821 - 1880)

APRIL 22

Goodbye, Maggie. Stay as sweet as you are. Goodbye, Lisa. I know you'll make me proud. Goodbye, Bart. ... I like your sheets.

>Homer Simpson

I keep the subject of my inquiry constantly before me, and wait till the first dawning opens gradually, by little and little, into a full and clear light.

>Isaac Newton (1642 - 1727)

Everything is vague to a degree you do not realize till you have tried to make it precise.

>Bertrand Russell (1872 - 1970)

Ah! Memory impairment: the free prize at the bottom of every vodka bottle!

>Chuck Lorre, Steven Molaro and Eric Kaplan

APRIL 23

Life does not cease to be funny when people die any more than it ceases to be serious when people laugh.

> George Bernard Shaw
> (1856 - 1950)

The most merciful thing in the world, I think, is the inability of the human mind to correlate all its contents.

> H. P. Lovecraft (1890 - 1937)

There ought to be one day-- just one-- when there is open season on senators.

> Will Rogers (1879 - 1935)

But in this world nothing can be said to be certain, except death and taxes.

> Benjamin Franklin
> (1706 - 1790)

APRIL 24

Can't this town go one day without a riot?

> Joe Quimby

Three o'clock is always too late or too early for anything you want to do.

> Jean-Paul Sartre (1905 - 1980)

No one who cannot rejoice in the discovery of his own mistakes deserves to be called a scholar.

> Donald Foster

Anybody can sympathise with the sufferings of a friend, but it requires a very fine nature to sympathise with a friend's success.

> Oscar Wilde (1854 - 1900)

APRIL 25

Money is better than poverty, if only for financial reasons.

> Woody Allen (1935 -)

Most people ignore most poetry because most poetry ignores most people.

> Adrian Mitchell

On the Internet, nobody knows you're a dog.

> Peter Steiner

An education isn't how much you have committed to memory, or even how much you know. It's being able to differentiate between what you do know and what you don't.

> Anatole France
> (1844 - 1924)

APRIL 26

Duct tape is like the force. It has a light side, a dark side, and it holds the universe together....

                      Carl Zwanzig

After all is said and done, a lot more will be said than done.

                      Unknown

Count Hermann Keyserling once said truly that the greatest American superstition was belief in facts.

                      John Gunther (1901 - 1970)

They used to photograph Shirley Temple through gauze. They should photograph me through linoleum.

                      Tallulah Bankhead (1903 - 1968)

APRIL 27

A fellow who is always declaring he's no fool usually has his suspicions.

>Wilson Mizner (1876 - 1933)

Eagles may soar, but weasels don't get sucked into jet engines.

>John Benfield

California is a fine place to live--if you happen to be an orange.

>Fred Allen (1894 - 1956)

The good psychic would pick up the phone before it rang. Of course it is possible there was noone on the other line. Once she said "God Bless you" I said, "I didn't sneeze" She looked deep into my eyes and said, "You will, eventually." And damn it if she wasn't right. Two days later I sneezed.

>Ellen DeGeneres

APRIL 28

As you journey through life take a minute every now and then to give a thought for the other fellow. He could be plotting something.

> Hagar the Horrible

I must take issue with the term 'a mere child,' for it has been my invariable experience that the company of a mere child is infinitely preferable to that of a mere adult.

> Fran Lebowitz (1950 -)

A man's respect for law and order exists in precise relationship to the size of his paycheck.

> Adam Clayton Powell Jr.
> (1908 - 1972)

We live in a society exquisitely dependent on science and technology, in which hardly anyone knows anything about science and technology.

> Carl Sagan (1934 - 1996)

APRIL 29

A vacuum is a hell of a lot better than some of the stuff that nature replaces it with.

> Tennessee Williams (1911 - 1983)

The secret to creativity is knowing how to hide your sources.

> Albert Einstein (1879 - 1955)

Not only is the universe stranger than we imagine, it is stranger than we can imagine.

> Sir Arthur Eddington
> (1882 - 1944)

The best way out is always through.

> Robert Frost (1874 - 1963)

APRIL 30

Suburbia is where the developer bulldozes out the trees, then names the streets after them.

> Bill Vaughan

Humor is just another defense against the universe.

> Mel Brooks (1926 -)

There is no such thing as "fun for the whole family."

> Jerry Seinfeld (1954 -)

Most people would rather be certain they're miserable than risk being happy.

> Robert Anthony

MAY 1

It is impossible to enjoy idling thoroughly unless one has plenty of work to do.

> Jerome K. Jerome
> (1859 - 1927)

I believe that banking institutions are more dangerous to our liberties than standing armies.

> Thomas Jefferson
> (1743 - 1826)

No good deed goes unpunished.

> Clare Booth Luce
> (1903 - 1987)

Grover Cleveland spanked me on two non-consecutive occasions.

> Abraham Simpson

MAY 2

There is nothing so absurd but some philosopher has said it.

> Cicero (106 BC - 43 BC)

It's no longer a question of staying healthy. It's a question of finding a sickness you like.

> Jackie Mason (1934 -)

A thought is often original, though you have uttered it a hundred times.

> Oliver Wendell Holmes
> (1809 - 1894)

The upper classes are... a nation's past; the middle class is its future.

> Ayn Rand (1905 - 1982)

MAY 3

It is no measure of health to be well adjusted to a profoundly sick society.

>Krishnamurti

A painting in a museum hears more ridiculous opinions than anything else in the world.

>Edmond de Goncourt
>(1822 - 1896)

You can fool some of the people all of the time, and all of the people some of the time, but you can not fool all of the people all of the time.

>Abraham Lincoln
>(1809 - 1865)

A man can stand anything except a succession of ordinary days.

>Johann Wolfgang von Goethe
>(1749 - 1832)

MAY 4

It's all right letting yourself go as long as you can let yourself back.

> Mick Jagger (1943 -)

You get fifteen democrats in a room, and you get twenty opinions.

> Senator Patrick Leahy (1940 -)

Unprovided with original learning, unformed in the habits of thinking, unskilled in the arts of composition, I resolved to write a book.

> Edward Gibbon (1737 - 1794)

I have long been of the opinion that if work were such a splendid thing the rich would have kept more of it for themselves.

> Bruce Grocott (1940 -)

MAY 5

To be willing to die for an idea is to set a rather high price on conjecture.

> Anatole France (1844 - 1924)

The truth is more important than the facts.

> Frank Lloyd Wright (1869 - 1959)

Excess on occasion is exhilarating. It prevents moderation from acquiring the deadening effect of a habit.

> W. Somerset Maugham
> (1874 - 1965)

They always talk who never think.

> Matthew Prior (1664 - 1721)

MAY 6

Some things have to be believed to be seen.

> Ralph Hodgson

Nothing fixes a thing so intensely in the memory as the wish to forget it.

> Michel de Montaigne
> (1533 - 1592)

Everyone has a purpose in life. Perhaps yours is watching television.

> David Letterman (1947 -)

To get something done, a committee should consist of no more than three men, two of whom are absent.

> Robert Copeland

MAY 7

An undefined problem has an infinite number of solutions.

> Robert A. Humphrey

The public will believe anything, so long as it is not founded on truth.

> Edith Sitwell (1887 - 1964)

Between your genius and my nothing we make a great team, come on give me a hug!

> Homer Simpson

You need only reflect that one of the best ways to get yourself a reputation as a dangerous citizen these days is to go about repeating the very phrases which our founding fathers used in the struggle for independence.

> Charles Austin Beard
> (1874 - 1948)

MAY 8

Half our life is spent trying to find something to do with the time we have rushed through life trying to save.

> Will Rogers (1879 - 1935)

Nothing is so admirable in politics as a short memory.

> John Kenneth Galbraith
> (1908 - 2006)

America is a large, friendly dog in a very small room. Every time it wags its tail, it knocks over a chair.

> Arnold Toynbee (1889 - 1975)

When a stupid man is doing something he is ashamed of, he always declares that it is his duty.

> George Bernard Shaw
> (1856 - 1950)

MAY 9

We've heard that a million monkeys at a million keyboards could produce the complete works of Shakespeare; now, thanks to the Internet, we know that is not true.

Robert Wilensky

Far from idleness being the root of all evil, it is rather the only true good.

Soren Kierkegaard
(1813 - 1855)

The most common of all follies is to believe passionately in the palpably not true. It is the chief occupation of mankind.

H. L. Mencken (1880 - 1956)

The grass is always greener once you don't have to mow a lawn anymore.

Randy K. Milholland

MAY 10

A boy can learn a lot from a dog: obedience, loyalty, and the importance of turning around three times before lying down.

> Robert Benchley (1889 - 1945)

Cogito cogito ergo cogito sum (I think that I think, therefore I think that I am.)

> Ambrose Bierce (1842 - 1914)

I believe that a scientist looking at nonscientific problems is just as dumb as the next guy.

> Richard Feynman (1918 - 1988)

The height of cleverness is to be able to conceal it.

> Francois de La Rochefoucauld
> (1613 - 1680)

MAY 11

Few things are harder to put up with than the annoyance of a good example.

Mark Twain (1835 - 1910)

Some people like my advice so much that they frame it upon the wall instead of using it.

Gordon R. Dickson

Idealism is what precedes experience; cynicism is what follows.

David T. Wolf (1943 -)

The most dangerous strategy is to jump a chasm in two leaps.

Benjamin Disraeli (1804 - 1881)

MAY 12

The only reason some people get lost in thought is because it's unfamiliar territory.

                                              Paul Fix

We are inclined to believe those whom we do not know because they have never deceived us.

                Samuel Johnson (1709 - 1784)

Most men are within a finger's breadth of being mad.

                              Diogenes the Cynic
                              (412 BC - 323 BC)

One thing you will probably remember well is any time you forgive and forget.

                              Franklin P. Jones

MAY 13

This isn't right. This isn't even wrong.
>Wolfgang Pauli (1900 - 1958)

Why isn't there a special name for the tops of your feet?
>Lily Tomlin (1939 -)

There are people who think that everything one does with a serious face is sensible.
>Georg Christoph Lichtenberg (1742 - 1799)

If the only tool you have is a hammer, you tend to see every problem as a nail.
>Abraham Maslow (1908 - 1970)

MAY 14

There are more pleasant things to do than beat up people.

> Muhammad Ali (1942 -)

Never attribute to malice what can be adequately explained by stupidity.

> Unknown

It is dangerous for a national candidate to say things that people might remember.

> Eugene McCarthy (1916 - 2005)

One of the few good things about modern times: If you die horribly on television, you will not have died in vain. You will have entertained us.

> Kurt Vonnegut (1922 - 2007)

MAY 15

Computers can figure out all kinds of problems, except the things in the world that just don't add up.

> James Magary

Man is tormented by no greater anxiety than to find someone quickly to whom he can hand over that great gift of freedom with which the ill-fated creature is born.

> Fyodor Dostoevsky (1821 - 1881), "The Brothers Karamazov"

Freedom of the press is limited to those who own one.

> A. J. Liebling (1904 - 1963)

One man alone can be pretty dumb sometimes, but for real bona fide stupidity, there ain't nothin' can beat teamwork.

> Edward Abbey (1927 - 1989)

MAY 16

It is possible to store the mind with a million facts and still be entirely uneducated.

> Alec Bourne

It's a rare person who wants to hear what he doesn't want to hear.

> Dick Cavett (1936 -)

If people never did silly things, nothing intelligent would ever get done.

> Ludwig Wittgenstein
> (1889 - 1951)

I'm a godmother, that's a great thing to be, a godmother. She calls me god for short, that's cute, I taught her that.

> Ellen DeGeneres

MAY 17

Hindsight is always twenty-twenty.
>Billy Wilder (1906 - 2002)

God made everything out of nothing, but the nothingness shows through.
>Paul Valery (1871 - 1945)

Advice to writers: Sometimes you just have to stop writing. Even before you begin.
>Stanislaw J. Lec (1909 - 1966)

There is no abstract art. You must always start with something. Afterward you can remove all traces of reality.
>Pablo Picasso (1881 - 1973)

MAY 18

War is much too serious a matter to be entrusted to the military.

> Georges Clemenceau
> (1841 - 1929)

A conference is a gathering of important people who singly can do nothing, but together can decide that nothing can be done.

> Fred Allen (1894 - 1956)

The only time to buy these is on a day with no 'y' in it.

> Warren Buffett (1930 -)

Fish is the only food that is considered spoiled once it smells like what it is.

> P. J. O'Rourke (1947 -)

MAY 19

Without the aid of prejudice and custom I should not be able to find my way across the room.

> William Hazlitt (1778 - 1830)

The saying "Getting there is half the fun" became obsolete with the advent of commercial airlines.

> Henry J. Tillman

There is a tragic flaw in our precious Constitution, and I don't know what can be done to fix it. This is it: Only nut cases want to be president.

> Kurt Vonnegut (1922 - 2007)

If you have any doubts that we live in a society controlled by men, try reading down the index of contributors to a volume of quotations, looking for women's names.

> Elaine Gill

MAY 20

People who throw kisses are hopelessly lazy.

> Bob Hope (1903 - 2003)

Every woman should have four pets in her life. A mink in her closet, a jaguar in her garage, a tiger in her bed, and a jackass who pays for everything.

> Paris Hilton

When Solomon said there was a time and a place for everything he had not encountered the problem of parking his automobile.

> Bob Edwards

Well, I hope you've learnt your lesson, Lisa: never help anyone.

> Homer Simpson

MAY 21

It is not enough to succeed. Others must fail.

> Gore Vidal (1925 -)

There are times when parenthood seems nothing but feeding the mouth that bites you.

> Peter De Vries

Silly is you in a natural state, and serious is something you have to do until you can get silly again.

> Mike Myers

It is better to deserve honors and not have them than to have them and not to deserve them.

> Mark Twain (1835 - 1910)

MAY 22

A kleptomaniac is a person who helps himself because he can't help himself.

>Henry Morgan

To achieve the impossible dream, try going to sleep.

>Joan Klempner

The radical of one century is the conservative of the next. The radical invents the views. When he has worn them out the conservative adopts them.

>Mark Twain (1835 - 1910)

To see what is in front of one's nose needs a constant struggle.

>George Orwell (1903 - 1950)

MAY 23

If I were two-faced, would I be wearing this one?
>Abraham Lincoln (1809 - 1865)

It's a small world, but I wouldn't want to paint it.
>Steven Wright (1955 -)

Remember that as a teenager you are at the last stage of your life when you will be happy to hear that the phone is for you.
>Fran Lebowitz (1950 -)

If you're not scared or angry at the thought of a human brain being controlled remotely, then it could be this prototype of mine is finally starting to work.
>John Alejandro King

MAY 24

In films murders are always very clean. I show how difficult it is and what a messy thing it is to kill a man.

>Alfred Hitchcock (1899 - 1980)

Well, we have no witnesses, no suspects, and no leads. If anyone has any information, please dial "0" and ask for the police. That number again, "0."

>Clarence Wiggum

Transported to a surreal landscape, a young girl kills the first woman she meets and then teams up with three complete strangers to kill again.

>Rick Polito

A lifetime of happiness! No man alive could bear it: it would be hell on earth.

>George Bernard Shaw
>(1856 - 1950)

MAY 25

Opportunity is missed by most people because it is dressed in overalls and looks like work.

Thomas A. Edison
(1847 - 1931)

Everyone thinks of changing the world, but no one thinks of changing himself.

Leo Tolstoy (1828 - 1910)

For most folks, no news is good news; for the press, good news is not news.

Gloria Borger

One never notices what has been done; one can only see what remains to be done.

Marie Curie (1867 - 1934)

MAY 26

They say that God is everywhere, and yet we always think of Him as somewhat of a recluse.
>Emily Dickinson (1830 - 1886)

Happiness is nothing more than good health and a bad memory.
>Albert Schweitzer (1875 - 1965)

Everyone is as God has made him, and oftentimes a great deal worse.
>Miguel de Cervantes (1547 - 1616)

Cynically speaking, one could say that it is true to life to be cynical about it.
>Paul Tillich (1886 - 1965)

MAY 27

I don't know if God exists, but it would be better for His reputation if He didn't.

> Jules Renard (1864 - 1910)

Never give a party if you will be the most interesting person there.

> Mickey Friedman

A good relationship is like fireworks: loud, explosive, and liable to maim you if you hold on too long.

> Jeph Jacques

There is no good lighting that is healthy and for our well being without proper darkness.

> Roger van der Heide

MAY 28

My problem lies in reconciling my gross habits with my net income.

> Errol Flynn (1909 - 1959)

When two men in business always agree, one of them is unnecessary.

> William Wrigley Jr. (1861 - 1932)

A bookstore is one of the only pieces of evidence we have that people are still thinking.

> Jerry Seinfeld (1954 -)

I grew up in Europe, where the history comes from.

> Eddie Izzard

MAY 29

The only thing I like about rich people is their money.

> Nancy Astor (1879 - 1964)

The multitude of books is making us ignorant.

> Voltaire (1694 - 1778)

Violence is the last refuge of the incompetent.

> Isaac Asimov (1920 - 1992)

A pessimist sees only the dark side of the clouds, and mopes; a philosopher sees both sides, and shrugs; an optimist doesn't see the clouds at all - he's walking on them.

> Leonard Louis Levinson

MAY 30

Famous remarks are very seldom quoted correctly.

> Simeon Strunsky (1879 - 1948)

Experience is the name everyone gives to their mistakes.

> Oscar Wilde (1854 - 1900)

I love quotations because it is a joy to find thoughts one might have, beautifully expressed with much authority by someone recognized wiser than oneself.

> Marlene Dietrich (1901 - 1992)

Whoever saw old age that did not applaud the past and condemn the present?

> Michel de Montaigne (1533 - 1592)

MAY 31

I don't know anything about music. In my line you don't have to.

> Elvis Presley (1935 - 1977)

Glory is fleeting, but obscurity is forever.

> Napoleon Bonaparte
> (1769 - 1821)

Lawyers spend a great deal of their time shoveling smoke.

> Oliver Wendell Holmes Jr.
> (1841 - 1935)

We hang the petty thieves and appoint the great ones to public office.

> Aesop (620 BC - 560 BC)

JUNE 1

Sometime they'll give a war and nobody will come.

>Carl Sandburg (1878 - 1967)

Bones heal, chicks dig scars, and the United States of America has the best doctor-to-daredevil ratio in the world.

>Lance Murdoch

In times like these, it helps to recall that there have always been times like these.

>Paul Harvey

The world is full of people whose notion of a satisfactory future is, in fact, a return to the idealised past.

>Robertson Davies

JUNE 2

People seem to enjoy things more when they know a lot of other people have been left out of the pleasure.

>Russell Baker (1925 -)

All things are difficult before they are easy.

>Dr. Thomas Fuller
>(1654 - 1734)

Before a war military science seems a real science, like astronomy; but after a war it seems more like astrology.

>Rebecca West (1892 - 1983)

Kids are like buckets of disease that live in your house.

>Louis C. K.

JUNE 3

The hardest thing in the world to understand is the income tax.

> Albert Einstein (1879 - 1955)

In the beginning the Universe was created. This has made a lot of people very angry and has been widely regarded as a bad move.

> Douglas Adams (1952 - 2001)

The price one pays for pursuing any profession or calling is an intimate knowledge of its ugly side.

> James Baldwin (1924 - 1987)

History is more or less bunk.

> Henry Ford (1863 - 1947)

JUNE 4

You can't say that civilization don't advance, however, for in every war they kill you in a new way.

> Will Rogers (1879 - 1935)

Conscience is the inner voice that warns us somebody may be looking.

> H. L. Mencken (1880 - 1956)

The reason there is so little crime in Germany is that it's against the law.

> Alex Levin

With or without religion, you would have good people doing good things and evil people doing evil things. But for good people to do evil things, that takes religion.

> Steven Weinberg (1933 -)

JUNE 5

An incompetent attorney can delay a trial for months or years. A competent attorney can delay one even longer.

> Evelle J. Younger

My life has no purpose, no direction, no aim, no meaning, and yet I'm happy. I can't figure it out. What am I doing right?

> Charles M. Schulz (1922 - 2000)

I'm thirty years old, but I read at the thirty-four-year-old level.

> Dana Carvey (1955 -)

Because things are the way they are, things will not stay the way they are.

> Bertolt Brecht (1898 - 1956)

JUNE 6

To invent, you need a good imagination and a pile of junk.

> Thomas A. Edison
> (1847 - 1931)

Fig Newton: The force required to accelerate a fig 39.37 inches per sec.

> J. Hart (1931 -)

If you can find something everyone agrees on, it's wrong.

> Mo Udall

I'm not going to live in a house of evil just to save a few dollars!

> Marge Simpson

JUNE 7

How can I believe in God when just last week I got my tongue caught in the roller of an electric typewriter?

>Woody Allen (1935 -)

Nothing so fortifies a friendship as a belief on the part of one friend that he is superior to the other.

>Honore de Balzac (1799 - 1850)

Silence is one of the hardest arguments to refute.

>Josh Billings (1818 - 1885)

Fanaticism consists in redoubling your effort when you have forgotten your aim.

>George Santayana (1863 - 1952)

JUNE 8

The young have aspirations that never come to pass, the old have reminiscences of what never happened.

> Saki (1870 - 1916)

You have to know how to accept rejection and reject acceptance.

> Ray Bradbury (1920 -)

The belief in a supernatural source of evil is not necessary; men alone are quite capable of every wickedness.

> Joseph Conrad (1857 - 1924)

Home is where the heart is, so your real home's in your chest.

> Joss Whedon, Zack Whedon,
> Maurissa Tancharoen,
> and Jed Whedon

JUNE 9

Power corrupts. Absolute power is kind of neat.

> John Lehman (1942 -)

After one look at this planet any visitor from outer space would say "I want to see the manager."

> William S. Burroughs
> (1914 - 1997)

That which has always been accepted by everyone, everywhere, is almost certain to be false.

> Paul Valery (1871 - 1945)

The glory of great men should always be measured by the means they have used to acquire it.

> Francois de La Rochefoucauld
> (1613 - 1680)

JUNE 10

Eternity is a mere moment, just long enough for a joke.

>Hermann Hesse (1877 - 1962)

A hypocrite is a person who--but who isn't?

>Don Marquis (1878 - 1937)

Reality is the leading cause of stress amongst those in touch with it.

>Jane Wagner

I think that somehow, we learn who we really are and then live with that decision.

>Eleanor Roosevelt (1884 - 1962)

JUNE 11

The aging process has you firmly in its grasp if you never get the urge to throw a snowball.

> Doug Larson

If little else, the brain is an educational toy.

> Tom Robbins (1936 -)

Most human beings have an almost infinite capacity for taking things for granted.

> Aldous Huxley (1894 - 1963)

There is no fate that cannot be surmounted by scorn.

> Albert Camus (1913 - 1960)

JUNE 12

Either this man is dead or my watch has stopped.

    Groucho Marx (1890 - 1977)

Until you've lost your reputation, you never realize what a burden it was.

    Margaret Mitchell (1900 - 1949)

You may find his accent peculiar. Certain aspects of his culture may seem absurd, perhaps even offensive. But I urge you all to give little Adil the benefit of the doubt. In this way, and only this way, can we hope to better understand our backward neighbors throughout the world.

    Seymour Skinner

I have the worst memory ever so no matter who comes up to me - they're just, like, 'I can't believe you don't remember me!" I'm like, 'Oh Dad I'm sorry!'

    Ellen DeGeneres

JUNE 13

To err is human--and to blame it on a computer is even more so.

> Robert Orben

For most of history, Anonymous was a woman.

> Virginia Woolf (1882 - 1941)

The stupid neither forgive nor forget; the naive forgive and forget; the wise forgive but do not forget.

> Thomas Szasz

The problem with the designated driver program, it's not a desirable job, but if you ever get sucked into doing it, have fun with it. At the end of the night, drop them off at the wrong house.

> Jeff Foxworthy

JUNE 14

I don't even butter my bread. I consider that cooking.

> Katherine Cebrian

America is a country that doesn't know where it is going but is determined to set a speed record getting there.

> Laurence J. Peter (1919 - 1988)

A foolish consistency is the hobgoblin of little minds, adored by little statesmen and philosophers and divines.

> Ralph Waldo Emerson
> (1803 - 1882)

In preparing for battle I have always found that plans are useless, but planning is indispensable.

> Dwight D. Eisenhower
> (1890 - 1969)

JUNE 15

Asking a working writer what he thinks about critics is like asking a lamppost how it feels about dogs.

> Christopher Hampton

The world is a tragedy to those who feel, but a comedy to those who think.

> Horace Walpole (1717 - 1797)

There are two ways to slide easily through life; to believe everything or to doubt everything. Both ways save us from thinking.

> Alfred Korzybski (1879 - 1950)

When one admits that nothing is certain one must, I think, also admit that some things are much more nearly certain than others.

> Bertrand Russell (1872 - 1970)

JUNE 16

I think the world is run by 'C' students.

> Al McGuire

It is only possible to live happily ever after on a day-to-day basis.

> Margaret Bonnano

America's one of the finest countries anyone ever stole.

> Bobcat Goldthwaite

A fashion is nothing but an induced epidemic.

> George Bernard Shaw
> (1856 - 1950)

JUNE 17

Football is a mistake. It combines the two worst elements of American life. Violence and committee meetings.

> George F. Will (1941 -)

I loathe people who keep dogs. They are cowards who haven't got the guts to bite people themselves.

> August Strindberg (1849 - 1912)

Much of the social history of the Western world over the past three decades has involved replacing what worked with what sounded good.

> Thomas Sowell (1930 -)

[Detractors] are just wrong, and that's okay. They just don't see it yet. That's what I would tell myself to keep those moments of doubt, only moments.

> Lisa Kudrow

JUNE 18

If Beethoven had been killed in a plane crash at the age of 22, it would have changed the history of music... and of aviation.

> Tom Stoppard (1937 -)

When I was younger, I could remember anything, whether it had happened or not.

> Mark Twain (1835 - 1910)

To have a right to do a thing is not at all the same as to be right in doing it.

> G. K. Chesterton (1874 - 1936)

Times have not become more violent. They have just become more televised.

> Marilyn Manson (1969 -)

JUNE 19

Stoop and you'll be stepped on; stand tall and you'll be shot at.

>Carlos A. Urbizo

I think on-stage nudity is disgusting, shameful and damaging to all things American. But if I were 22 with a great body, it would be artistic, tasteful, patriotic and a progressive religious experience.

>Shelley Winters (1922 - 2006)

Courage is the art of being the only one who knows you're scared to death.

>Harold Wilson (1916 - 1995)

When I came back to Dublin I was courtmartialed in my absence and sentenced to death in my absence, so I said they could shoot me in my absence.

>Brendan Behan (1923 - 1964)

JUNE 20

It is impossible to travel faster than the speed of light, and certainly not desirable, as one's hat keeps blowing off.

                        Woody Allen (1935 -)

Never knock on Death's door: ring the bell and run away! Death really hates that!

                        Matt Frewer

You might remember me from such self-help videos as "Smoke Yourself Thin" and "Get Confident, Stupid."

                        Troy McClure

There are painters who transform the sun to a yellow spot, but there are others who with the help of their art and their intelligence, transform a yellow spot into the sun.

                        Pablo Picasso (1881 - 1973)

JUNE 21

A cucumber should be well-sliced, dressed with pepper and vinegar, and then thrown out.

> Samuel Johnson (1709 - 1784)

I never vote for anyone; I always vote against.

> W. C. Fields (1880 - 1946)

The best liar is he who makes the smallest amount of lying go the longest way.

> Samuel Butler (1835 - 1902)

We never stop investigating. We are never satisfied that we know enough to get by. Every question we answer leads on to another question. This has become the greatest survival trick of our species.

> Desmond Morris

JUNE 22

A wise man gets more use from his enemies than a fool from his friends.

> Baltasar Gracian

'Tis an ill wind that blows no minds.

> Malaclypse the Younger

Not a shred of evidence exists in favor of the idea that life is serious.

> Brendan Gill

The conventional view serves to protect us from the painful job of thinking.

> John Kenneth Galbraith
> (1908 - 2006)

JUNE 23

I'm as pure as the driven slush.

>Tallulah Bankhead (1903 - 1968)

Ahh, now to spend some quality time away from my family.

>Homer Simpson

Give me the luxuries of life and I will willingly do without the necessities.

>Frank Lloyd Wright
>(1869 - 1959)

I only know two pieces; one is 'Clair de Lune' and the other one isn't.

>Victor Borge (1909 - 2000)

JUNE 24

No.

> Amy Carter

Everybody gets so much information all day long that they lose their common sense.

> Gertrude Stein (1874 - 1946)

A signature always reveals a man's character - and sometimes even his name.

> Evan Esar (1899 - 1995)

I've done the calculation and your chances of winning the lottery are identical whether you play or not.

> Fran Lebowitz (1950 -)

JUNE 25

If all the cars in the United States were placed end to end, it would probably be Labor Day Weekend.

> Doug Larson

Marge, I can't wear a pink shirt to work. Everybody wears white shirts. I'm not popular enough to be different!

> Homer Simpson

Civilization is the process of reducing the infinite to the finite.

> Oliver Wendell Holmes
> (1809 - 1894)

Perhaps the most valuable result of all education is the ability to make yourself do the thing you have to do, when it ought to be done, whether you like it or not.

> Thomas Henry Huxley

JUNE 26

There is a coherent plan in the universe, though I don't know what it's a plan for.

> Fred Hoyle (1915 - 2001)

A neurosis is a secret that you don't know you are keeping.

> Kenneth Tynan

Maturity is a bitter disappointment for which no remedy exists, unless laughter can be said to remedy anything.

> Kurt Vonnegut (1922 - 2007)

There are a terrible lot of lies going around the world, and the worst of it is half of them are true.

> Sir Winston Churchill
> (1874 - 1965)

JUNE 27

Imitation is the sincerest form of television.

>Fred Allen (1894 - 1956)

You must not think me necessarily foolish because I am facetious, nor will I consider you necessarily wise because you are grave.

>Sydney Smith (1771 - 1845)

Contrary to general belief, I do not believe that friends are necessarily the people you like best, they are merely the people who got there first.

>Peter Ustinov (1921 - 2004)

When you look at yourself from a universal standpoint, something inside always reminds or informs you that there are bigger and better things to worry about.

>Albert Einstein (1879 - 1955)

JUNE 28

I am not sincere, even when I say I am not.

> Jules Renard (1864 - 1910)

Listening, not imitation, may be the sincerest form of flattery.

> Dr. Joyce Brothers (1928 -)

What you do speaks so loud that I cannot hear what you say.

> Ralph Waldo Emerson
> (1803 - 1882)

A little government and a little luck are necessary in life, but only a fool trusts either of them.

> P. J. O'Rourke (1947 -)

JUNE 29

I've gone into hundreds of [fortune-teller's parlors], and have been told thousands of things, but nobody ever told me I was a policewoman getting ready to arrest her.

>> New York City detective

Oh "meltdown". That's one of those annoying buzz words. We prefer to call it an un-requested fission surplus.

>> Montgomery Burns

I have not failed. I've just found 10,000 ways that won't work.

> Thomas A. Edison (1847 - 1931)

Idleness is not doing nothing. Idleness is being free to do anything.

>> Floyd Dell

JUNE 30

2 is not equal to 3, not even for large values of 2.

> Grabel's Law

It is bad luck to be superstitious.

> Andrew W. Mathis

Dealing with network executives is like being nibbled to death by ducks.

> Eric Sevareid

The middle of the road is where the white line is-and that's the worst place to drive.

> Robert Frost (1874 - 1963)

JULY 1

Life is what happens to you while you're busy making other plans.

> John Lennon (1940 - 1980)

In theory, there is no difference between theory and practice; In practice, there is.

> Chuck Reid

The avoidance of taxes is the only intellectual pursuit that carries any reward.

> John Maynard Keynes
> (1883 - 1946)

The true measure of a man is how he treats someone who can do him absolutely no good.

> Samuel Johnson (1709 - 1784)

JULY 2

Until you walk a mile in another man's moccasins you can't imagine the smell.
> Robert Byrne

All that is human must retrograde if it does not advance.
> Edward Gibbon (1737 - 1794)

There is only one thing a philosopher can be relied upon to do, and that is to contradict other philosophers.
> William James (1842 - 1910)

Never harbor grudges; they sour your stomach and do no harm to anyone else.
> Robertson Davies

JULY 3

Time flies like an arrow. Fruit flies like a banana.
>Groucho Marx (1890 - 1977)

You are not superior just because you see the world in an odious light.
>Vicomte de Chateaubriand
>(1768 - 1848)

Washington is a city of Southern efficiency and Northern charm.
>John F. Kennedy (1917 - 1963)

An ounce of action is worth a ton of theory.
>Friedrich Engels (1820 - 1895)

JULY 4

J.F.K.--The Man and the Airport
> Unknown

One machine can do the work of fifty ordinary men. No machine can do the work of one extraordinary man.
> Elbert Hubbard (1856 - 1915)

Sometimes I've believed as many as six impossible things before breakfast.
> Lewis Carroll (1832 - 1898)

One of the indictments of civilizations is that happiness and intelligence are so rarely found in the same person.
> William Feather (1908 - 1976)

JULY 5

By the time we've made it, we've had it.

> Malcolm Forbes (1919 - 1990)

Confusion is always the most honest response.

> Marty Indik

How do you tell a communist? Well, it's someone who reads Marx and Lenin. And how do you tell an anti-Communist? It's someone who understands Marx and Lenin.

> Ronald Reagan (1911 - 2004)

Feed a fever, starve a cold. Lightly sup with rickets.

> Takayuki Ikkaku, Arisa Hosaka and Toshihiro Kawabata

JULY 6

A good novel tells us the truth about its hero; but a bad novel tells us the truth about its author.

> G. K. Chesterton (1874 - 1936)

If I knew I was going to live this long, I'd have taken better care of myself.

> Mickey Mantle (1931 - 1995)

He had discovered a great law of human action, without knowing it - namely, that in order to make a man or a boy covet a thing, it is only necessary to make the thing difficult to obtain.

> Mark Twain (1835 - 1910)

The only road to good shows is bad ones. Just go start having a bad time, and if you don't give up, you will get better.

> Louis C. K.

JULY 7

The best way to keep one's word is not to give it.

> Napoleon Bonaparte
> (1769 - 1821)

Life is a moderately good play with a badly written third act.

> Truman Capote (1924 - 1984)

In all recorded history there has not been one economist who has had to worry about where the next meal would come from.

> Peter Drucker (1909 - 2005)

If everything seems under control, you're not going fast enough

> Mario Andretti (1940 -)

JULY 8

You know everybody is ignorant, only on different subjects.

> Will Rogers (1879 - 1935)

If there is no God, who pops up the next Kleenex?

> Art Hoppe

Nobody talks so constantly about God as those who insist that there is no God.

> Heywood Broun (1888 - 1939)

Even he, to whom most things that most people would think were pretty smart were pretty dumb, thought it was pretty smart.

> Douglas Adams (1952 - 2001)

JULY 9

The great thing about democracy is that it gives every voter a chance to do something stupid.

> Art Spander

Every great advance in natural knowledge has involved the absolute rejection of authority.

> Thomas H. Huxley (1825 - 1895)

As I grow older , I regret to say that a detestable habit of thinking seems to be getting a hold of me.

> H. Rider Haggard (1856 - 1925)

I'm a jerk to everyone. Best way to protect yourself from lawsuits.

> David Hoselton

JULY 10

People find life entirely too time-consuming.

>Stanislaw J. Lec (1909 - 1966)

Laws are like sausages. It's better not to see them being made.

>Otto von Bismarck (1815 - 1898)

I like rice. Rice is great if you're hungry and want 2000 of something.

>Mitch Hedberg (1968 - 2005)

The trouble with weather forecasting is that it's right too often for us to ignore it and wrong too often for us to rely on it.

>Patrick Young

JULY 11

Oh boy, dinnertime. The perfect break between work and drunk!

>Homer Simpson

When people are free to do as they please, they usually imitate each other.

>Eric Hoffer (1902 - 1983)

Tact is the knack of making a point without making an enemy.

>Isaac Newton (1642 - 1727)

Just as I feared, her Buddhism has led directly to witchcraft.

>Ned Flanders

JULY 12

Well, if crime fighters fight crime and fire fighters fight fire, what do freedom fighters fight? They never mention that part to us, do they?

> George Carlin (1937 - 2008)

One doesn't have a sense of humor. It has you.

> Larry Gelbart

It only takes 20 years for a liberal to become a conservative without changing a single idea.

> Robert Anton Wilson

Life is just a bowl of pits.

> Rodney Dangerfield
> (1921 - 2004)

JULY 13

I stopped believing in Santa Claus when my mother took me to see him in a department store, and he asked for my autograph.

> Shirley Temple (1928 -)

Some weasel took the cork out of my lunch.

> W. C. Fields (1880 - 1946)

And that's the world in a nutshell, an appropriate receptacle.

> Stan Dunn

An economist is a surgeon with an excellent scalpel and a rough-edged lancet, who operates beautifully on the dead and tortures the living.

> Nicholas Chamfort (1741 - 1794)

JULY 14

I don't want any yes-men around me. I want everybody to tell me the truth even if it costs them their jobs.

> Samuel Goldwyn (1882 - 1974)

The scientific theory I like best is that the rings of Saturn are composed entirely of lost airline luggage.

> Mark Russell (1932 -)

All I have to say is: Jessica Simpson is the most beautiful woman on the planet!

> Jessica Simpson

Son, don't overreach. Go for the dented car, the dead-end job, the less attractive girl. I blame myself. I should have had this talk a long time ago.

> Abraham Simpson

JULY 15

There's no point in being grown up if you can't be childish sometimes.

> Doctor Who

With Epcot Center the Disney corporation has accomplished something I didn't think possible in today's world. They have created a land of make-believe that's worse than regular life.

> P. J. O'Rourke (1947 -)

The hardest thing to learn in life is which bridge to cross and which to burn.

> David Russell

Whatever you may be sure of, be sure of this, that you are dreadfully like other people.

> James Russell Lowell
> (1819 - 1891)

JULY 16

What can you say about a society that says that God is dead and Elvis is alive?

> Irv Kupcinet

It chose to destroy itself rather than live with us. You can't help but feel a little rejected.

> Lisa Simpson

Charm is a way of getting the answer yes without asking a clear question.

> Albert Camus (1913 - 1960)

A man can be happy with any woman as long as he does not love her.

> Oscar Wilde (1854 - 1900)

JULY 17

Our differences are only skin deep, but our sames go down to the bone.

> Marge Simpson

Part of being sane, is being a little bit crazy.

> Janet Long

The computing field is always in need of new cliches.

> Alan Perlis

What music is more enchanting than the voices of young people, when you can't hear what they say?

> Logan Pearsall Smith
> (1865 - 1946)

JULY 18

Today you can go to a gas station and find the cash register open and the toilets locked. They must think toilet paper is worth more than money.

>Joey Bishop (1918 -)

Two paradoxes are better than one; they may even suggest a solution.

>Edward Teller (1908 - 2003)

Well, he's kind of had it in for me ever since I accidently ran over his dog. Actually, replace "accidently" with "repeatedly," and replace "dog" with "son."

>Lionel Hutz

Get the facts, or the facts will get you. And when you get them, get them right, or they will get you wrong.

>Dr. Thomas Fuller
>(1654 - 1734)

JULY 19

It is easier to forgive an enemy than to forgive a friend.

>William Blake (1757 - 1827)

College isn't the place to go for ideas.

>Helen Keller (1880 - 1968)

To be a book-collector is to combine the worst characteristics of a dope fiend with those of a miser.

>Robertson Davies

The United States Congress, like a lot of rich people, lives in two houses.

>John Green

JULY 20

I don't have a bank account, because I don't know my mother's maiden name.

> Paula Poundstone

As an adolescent I aspired to lasting fame, I craved factual certainty, and I thirsted for a meaningful vision of human life - so I became a scientist. This is like becoming an archbishop so you can meet girls.

> M. Cartmill

Life is like playing a violin in public and learning the instrument as one goes on.

> Samuel Butler (1835 - 1902)

The petty economies of the rich are just as amazing as the silly extravagances of the poor.

> William Feather (1908 - 1976)

JULY 21

Classical music is the kind we keep thinking will turn into a tune.

> Kin Hubbard (1868 - 1930)

The opposite of talking isn't listening. The opposite of talking is waiting.

> Fran Lebowitz (1950 -)

No one can earn a million dollars honestly.

> William Jennings Bryan
> (1860 - 1925)

Facts are the enemy of truth.

> Miguel de Cervantes
> (1547 - 1616)

JULY 22

Lighten up ladies. It's not cheating if you're wearing a costume.

> Homer Simpson

Oh, come on. If you can't laugh at the walking dead, who can you laugh at?

> Unknown

Either I've been missing something or nothing has been going on.

> Karen Elizabeth Gordon

This is my favorite book in all the world, though I have never read it.

> William Goldman

JULY 23

I am prepared to meet my Maker. Whether my Maker is prepared for the great ordeal of meeting me is another matter.

Sir Winston Churchill
(1874 - 1965)

I improve on misquotation.

Cary Grant (1904 - 1986)

There is no pleasure in having nothing to do; the fun is in having lots to do and not doing it.

Mary Wilson Little

I gotta work out. I keep saying it all the time. I keep saying I gotta start working out. It's been about two months since I've worked out. And I just don't have the time. Which uh... is odd. Because I have the time to go out to dinner. And uh... and watch tv. And get a bone density test. And uh... try to figure out what my phone number spells in words.

Ellen DeGeneres

JULY 24

The whole problem can be stated quite simply by asking, 'Is there a meaning to music?' My answer would be, 'Yes.' And 'Can you state in so many words what the meaning is?' My answer to that would be, 'No.'

                Aaron Copland (1900 - 1990)

The more I want to get something done, the less I call it work.

                Richard Bach

Middle age is when you've met so many people that every new person you meet reminds you of someone else.

                Ogden Nash (1902 - 1971)

Drive-in banks were established so most of the cars today could see their real owners.

                E. Joseph Cossman

JULY 25

It has always been the prerogative of children and half-wits to point out that the emperor has no clothes. But the half-wit remains a half-wit, and the emperor remains an emperor.

Neil Gaiman

This goes against every feminist bone in my body, but Dad, can't you control your woman?

Lisa Simpson

Zoo: An excellent place to study the habits of human beings.

Evan Esar (1899 - 1995)

Shoplifting is a victimless crime. Like punching someone in the dark.

Nelson Muntz

JULY 26

Freedom is just Chaos, with better lighting.

> Alan Dean Foster

Those who would give up essential liberty to purchase a little temporary safety deserve neither liberty nor safety.

> Benjamin Franklin (1706 - 1790)

How vain it is to sit down to write when you have not stood up to live.

> Henry David Thoreau
> (1817 - 1862)

Sometimes people are layered like that. There's something totally different underneath than what's on the surface. But sometimes, there's a third, even deeper level, and that one is the same as the top surface one. Like with pie.

> Joss Whedon, Zack Whedon,
> Maurissa Tancharoen,
> and Jed Whedon

JULY 27

My doctor told me to stop having intimate dinners for four. Unless there are three other people.

> Orson Welles (1915 - 1985)

What we anticipate seldom occurs; what we least expected generally happens.

> Benjamin Disraeli (1804 - 1881)

Liberty without learning is always in peril; learning without liberty is always in vain.

> John F. Kennedy (1917 - 1963)

When a person can no longer laugh at himself, it is time for others to laugh at him.

> Thomas Szasz

JULY 28

I don't know the key to success, but the key to failure is trying to please everybody.

Bill Cosby (1937 -)

Most people are other people. Their thoughts are someone else's opinions, their lives a mimicry, their passions a quotation.

Oscar Wilde (1854 - 1900)

Nobody will ever win the Battle of the Sexes. There's just too much fraternizing with the enemy.

Henry Kissinger (1923 -)

Writing is the only profession where no one considers you ridiculous if you earn no money.

Jules Renard (1864 - 1910)

JULY 29

The Army has carried the American ... ideal to its logical conclusion. Not only do they prohibit discrimination on the grounds of race, creed and color, but also on ability.

> Tom Lehrer (1928 -)

My husband gave me a necklace. It's fake. I requested fake. Maybe I'm paranoid, but in this day and age, I don't want something around my neck that's worth more than my head.

> Rita Rudner

If history repeats itself, and the unexpected always happens, how incapable must Man be of learning from experience.

George Bernard Shaw (1856 - 1950)

Nothing has an uglier look to us than reason, when it is not on our side.

> Halifax

JULY 30

It is impossible to imagine Goethe or Beethoven being good at billiards or golf.

          H. L. Mencken (1880 - 1956)

Any great truth can -- and eventually will -- be expressed as a cliche -- a cliche is a sure and certain way to dilute an idea. For instance, my grandmother used to say, 'The black cat is always the last one off the fence.' I have no idea what she meant, but at one time, it was undoubtedly true.

          Solomon Short

Oil prices have fallen lately. We include this news for the benefit of gas stations, which otherwise wouldn't learn of it for six months.

          Bill Tammeus

Art, like morality, consists of drawing the line somewhere.

          G. K. Chesterton (1874 - 1936)

JULY 31

Me, fail English? That's unpossible.

> Ralph Wiggum

The statistics on sanity are that one out of every four Americans is suffering from some form of mental illness. Think of your three best friends. If they're okay, then it's you.

> Rita Mae Brown

Once the game is over, the King and the pawn go back in the same box.

> Italian Proverb

Music makes one feel so romantic - at least it always gets on one's nerves - which is the same thing nowadays.

> Oscar Wilde (1854 - 1900)

AUGUST 1

He who hesitates is a damned fool.

> Mae West (1892 - 1980)

Learning to dislike children at an early age saves a lot of expense and aggravation later in life.

> Robert Byrne

When a person cannot deceive himself the chances are against his being able to deceive other people.

> Mark Twain (1835 - 1910),
> Mark Twain's Autobiography

The time to relax is when you don't have time for it.

> Sydney J. Harris

AUGUST 2

Sure there are dishonest men in local government. But there are dishonest men in national government too.

>Richard M. Nixon (1913 - 1994)

The reason grandparents and grandchildren get along so well is that they have a common enemy.

>Sam Levenson (1911 - 1980)

Have the courage to be ignorant of a great number of things, in order to avoid the calamity of being ignorant of everything.

>Sydney Smith (1771 - 1845)

I'm sick of following my dreams. I'm just going to ask them where they're going and hook up with them later.

>Mitch Hedberg (1968 - 2005)

AUGUST 3

In these matters the only certainty is that nothing is certain.

> Pliny the Elder (23 AD - 79 AD)

No problem is so formidable that you can't walk away from it.

> Charles M. Schulz (1922 - 2000)

There is no such thing as an underestimate of average intelligence.

> Henry Adams (1838 - 1918)

Nobody knows the age of the human race, but everybody agrees that it is old enough to know better.

> Anonymous

AUGUST 4

Music is essentially useless, as life is.

> George Santayana (1863 - 1952)

One of the advantages of being disorderly is that one is constantly making exciting discoveries.

> A. A. Milne (1882 - 1956)

Why shouldn't things be largely absurd, futile, and transitory? They are so, and we are so, and they and we go very well together.

> George Santayana (1863 - 1952)

There is no reciprocity. Men love women, women love children, children love hamsters.

> Alice Thomas Ellis

AUGUST 5

People can have the Model T in any colour--so long as it's black.
>Henry Ford (1863 - 1947)

Every hero becomes a bore at last.
>Ralph Waldo Emerson
>(1803 - 1882)

Politics is not the art of the possible. It consists in choosing between the disastrous and the unpalatable.
>John Kenneth Galbraith
>(1908 - 2006)

I am certain there is too much certainty in the world.
>Michael Crichton (1942 - 2008)

AUGUST 6

Early to rise and early to bed makes a male healthy and wealthy and dead.

>James Thurber (1894 - 1961)

The great thing about human language is that it prevents us from sticking to the matter at hand.

>Lewis Thomas (1913 - 1993)

The desire to take medicine is perhaps the greatest feature which distinguishes man from animals.

>Sir William Osler (1849 - 1919)

I'm a great believer in luck, and I find the harder I work the more I have of it.

>Thomas Jefferson (1743 - 1826)

AUGUST 7

Let us make a special effort to stop communicating with each other, so we can have some conversation.

> Judith Martin

Play: Work that you enjoy doing for nothing.

> Evan Esar (1899 - 1995)

Equations are the devil's sentences.

> Stephen Colbert

Cocaine is God's way of saying that you're making too much money.

> Robin Williams (1951 -)

AUGUST 8

The optimist proclaims that we live in the best of all possible worlds; and the pessimist fears this is true.

James Branch Cabell (1879 - 1958)

People everywhere confuse what they read in newspapers with news.

A. J. Liebling (1904 - 1963)

Fat Tony is a cancer on this fair city. He is the cancer, and I am the...um...What cures cancer?

Clarence Wiggum

You know that children are growing up when they start asking questions that have answers.

John J. Plomp

AUGUST 9

The trouble with being punctual is that nobody's there to appreciate it.

>> Franklin P. Jones

Always and never are two words you should always remember never to use.

>> Wendell Johnson

Everyone has a right to a university degree in America, even if it's in Hamburger Technology.

>> Clive James

One should absorb the colour of life, but one should never remember its details. Details are always vulgar.

>> Oscar Wilde (1854 - 1900)

AUGUST 10

Sanity calms, but madness is more interesting.

> John Russell

Never judge a book by its movie.

> J. W. Eagan

People are always blaming their circumstances for what they are. I don't believe in circumstances. The people who get on in this world are the people who get up and look for the circumstances they want, and, if they can't find them, make them.

> George Bernard Shaw
> (1856 - 1950)

Late to bed and late to wake will keep you long on money and short on mistakes.

> Aaron McGruder

AUGUST 11

That is the saving grace of humor, if you fail no one is laughing at you.

A. Whitney Brown

Interestingly, according to modern astronomers, space is finite. This is a very comforting thought-- particularly for people who can never remember where they have left things.

Woody Allen (1935 -)

If there were in the world today any large number of people who desired their own happiness more than they desired the unhappiness of others, we could have paradise in a few years.

Bertrand Russell (1872 - 1970)

Priceless like a mother's love, or the good kind of priceless?

Bart Simpson

AUGUST 12

All the President is, is a glorified public relations man who spends his time flattering, kissing and kicking people to get them to do what they are supposed to do anyway.

                Harry S Truman (1884 - 1972)

I can picture in my mind a world without war, a world without hate. And I can picture us attacking that world, because they'd never expect it.

                      Jack Handey (1949 -)

The universal brotherhood of man is our most precious possession, what there is of it.

                  Mark Twain (1835 - 1910)

I'm glad I didn't have to fight in any war. I'm glad I didn't have to pick up a gun. I'm glad I didn't get killed or kill somebody. I hope my kids enjoy the same lack of manhood.

                      Tom Hanks (1956 -)

AUGUST 13

Ironic, isn't it, Smithers? This anonymous clan of slack-jawed troglodytes has cost me the election. And yet, if I were to have them killed, I would be the one to go to jail. That's democracy for you.

></br>Montgomery Burns

When we got into office, the thing that surprised me the most was that things were as bad as we'd been saying they were.

></br>John F. Kennedy (1917 - 1963)

The place where optimism most flourishes is the lunatic asylum.

></br>Havelock Ellis (1859 - 1939)

A synonym is a word you use when you can't spell the word you first thought of.

></br>Burt Bacharach (1928 -)

AUGUST 14

People that are really very weird can get into sensitive positions and have a tremendous impact on history.

>Dan Quayle (1947 -)

I shot an arrow into the air, and it stuck.

>Graffito

They say such nice things about people at their funerals that it makes me sad to realize that I'm going to miss mine by just a few days.

>Garrison Keillor (1942 -)

Lies are like children. If you don't nurture them, they'll never be useful later.

>Randy K. Milholland

AUGUST 15

I feel like a fugitive from the law of averages.

>William H. Mauldin (1921 - 2003)

A waist is a terrible thing to mind.

>Jane Caminos

Say what you will about the Ten Commandments, you must always come back to the pleasant fact that there are only ten of them.

>H. L. Mencken (1880 - 1956)

Humor is our way of defending ourselves from life's absurdities by thinking absurdly about them.

>Lewis Mumford (1895 - 1990)

AUGUST 16

A friend is someone who will help you move. A real friend is someone who will help you move a body.

> Unknown

The town where I grew up has a zip code of E-I-E-I-O.

> Martin Mull (1943 -)

We should be taught not to wait for inspiration to start a thing. Action always generates inspiration. Inspiration seldom generates action.

> Frank Tibolt

The phrase "action speaks louder than words," is most easily proven by a swift kick to the genitals.

> Devin J. Monroe (1983 -)

AUGUST 17

I like pigs. Dogs look up to us. Cats look down on us. Pigs treat us as equals.

  Sir Winston Churchill (1874 - 1965)

Never eat more than you can lift.

                             Miss Piggy

Under democracy one party always devotes its chief energies to trying to prove that the other party is unfit to rule - and both commonly succeed, and are right.

        H. L. Mencken (1880 - 1956)

There are two kinds of light--the glow that illuminates, and the glare that obscures.

        James Thurber (1894 - 1961)

AUGUST 18

Maturity is only a short break in adolescence.

> Jules Feiffer (1929 -)

To be pleased with one's limits is a wretched state.

> Johann Wolfgang von Goethe
> (1749 - 1832)

Never be afraid to laugh at yourself, after all, you could be missing out on the joke of the century.

> Dame Edna Everage (1934 -)

If we couldn't laugh, we would all go insane.

> Jimmy Buffett

AUGUST 19

The whole world is in revolt. Soon there will be only five Kings left--the King of England, the King of Spades, The King of Clubs, the King of Hearts, and the King of Diamonds.

> King Farouk of Egypt
> (1920 - 1965)

An expert is a person who avoids small error as he sweeps on to the grand fallacy.

> Benjamin Stolberg

A little nonsense now and then, is relished by the wisest men.

> Anonymous

Humanity is acquiring all the right technology for all the wrong reasons.

> R. Buckminster Fuller
> (1895 - 1983)

AUGUST 20

As for me, except for an occasional heart attack, I feel as young as I ever did.

> Robert Benchley (1889 - 1945)

I have a rock garden. Last week three of them died.

> Richard Diran

Reminds me of my safari in Africa. Somebody forgot the corkscrew and for several days we had to live on nothing but food and water.

> W. C. Fields (1880 - 1946)

Do not worry about your difficulties in Mathematics. I can assure you mine are still greater.

> Albert Einstein (1879 - 1955)

AUGUST 21

I think Superman should go on the Larry King show and announce that he would come back to life if people in all 50 states wanted him to.

> Dave Barry (1947 -)

I can think of nothing less pleasurable than a life devoted to pleasure.

> John D. Rockefeller
> (1839 - 1937)

Politics is supposed to be the second oldest profession. I have come to realize that it bears a very close resemblance to the first.

> Ronald Reagan (1911 - 2004)

The only function of economic forecasting is to make astrology look respectable.

> John Kenneth Galbraith
> (1908 - 2006)

AUGUST 22

The higher the buildings, the lower the morals.

> Noel Coward (1899 - 1973)

The only way to entertain some folks is to listen to them.

> Kin Hubbard (1868 - 1930)

Elections are won by men and women chiefly because most people vote against somebody rather than for somebody.

> Franklin P. Adams (1881 - 1960)

I don't care what it is, when it has an LCD screen, it makes it better.

> Kevin Rose

AUGUST 23

Ambition is a poor excuse for not having sense enough to be lazy.

                Edgar Bergen (1903 - 1978)

Drama is life with the dull bits cut out.

                Alfred Hitchcock (1899 - 1980)

I wish people who have trouble communicating would just shut up.

                Tom Lehrer (1928 -)

When a thing is funny, search it carefully for a hidden truth.

                George Bernard Shaw
                          (1856 - 1950)

AUGUST 24

I can't promise I'll try, but I'll try to try.

> Bart Simpson

In religion and politics, people's beliefs and convictions are in almost every case gotten at second hand, and without examination.

> Mark Twain (1835 - 1910)

Give a man a fish, and you'll feed him for a day. Teach a man to fish, and he'll buy a funny hat. Talk to a hungry man about fish, and you're a consultant.

> Scott Adams (1957 -)

Mothers may still want their sons to grow up to be President, but according to a famous Gallup poll of some years ago, some 73 percent do not want them to become politicians in the process.

> John F. Kennedy (1917 - 1963)

AUGUST 25

I would rather be a coward than brave because people hurt you when you are brave.

> E. M. Forster (1879 - 1970)

Thanks to the Interstate Highway System, it is now possible to travel from coast to coast without seeing anything.

> Charles Kuralt

Strange as it seems, no amount of learning can cure stupidity, and higher education positively fortifies it.

> Stephen Vizinczey

About the most originality that any writer can hope to achieve honestly is to steal with good judgment.

> Josh Billings (1818 - 1885)

AUGUST 26

I no longer prepare food or drink with more than one ingredient.

> Cyra McFadden

Bart, having never received any words of encouragement myself, I'm not sure how they're supposed to sound, but here goes. I believe in you.

> Lisa Simpson

We are more ready to try the untried when what we do is inconsequential. Hence the fact that many inventions had their birth as toys.

> Eric Hoffer (1902 - 1983)

The visionary lies to himself, the liar only to others.

> Friedrich Nietzsche
> (1844 - 1900)

AUGUST 27

The prime purpose of eloquence is to keep other people from talking.

> Louis Vermeil

Never face facts; if you do, you'll never get up in the morning.

> Marlo Thomas

There is scarcely anything in the world that some man cannot make a little worse, and sell a little more cheaply. The person who buys on price alone is this man's lawful prey.

> John Ruskin (1819 - 1900)

My marriage had its ups and downs like anyone's, but when it came down to it, I knew it was solid. I miss that sort of security, and that sort of connection with someone.

> John Scalzi

AUGUST 28

A nation is a society united by delusions about its ancestry and by common hatred of its neighbors.

> William Ralph Inge
> (1860 - 1954)

A child of five would understand this. Send someone to fetch a child of five.

> Groucho Marx (1890 - 1977)

There is always more misery among the lower classes than there is humanity in the higher.

> Victor Hugo (1802 - 1885)

The most erroneous stories are those we think we know best - and therefore never scrutinize or question.

> Stephen Jay Gould
> (1941 - 2002)

AUGUST 29

Democracy is the name we give the people whenever we need them.

>Marquis de Flers Robert
>and Arman de Caillavet

A rabbi would never exaggerate. A rabbi composes. He creates thoughts. He tells stories that may never have happened. But he does not exaggerate.

>Rabbi Krustofsky

The world's as ugly as sin, and almost as delightful

>Frederick Locker-Lampson

I once wanted to become an atheist, but I gave up - they have no holidays.

>Henny Youngman
>(1906 - 1998)

AUGUST 30

It is a very sad thing that nowadays there is so little useless information.

>Oscar Wilde (1854 - 1900)

Honest criticism is hard to take, particularly from a relative, a friend, an acquaintance, or a stranger.

>Franklin P. Jones

It's so much easier to suggest solutions when you don't know too much about the problem.

>Malcolm Forbes (1919 - 1990)

They wouldn't call it falling in love if you didn't get hurt sometimes, but you just pick yourself up and move on.

>Gregory Thomas Garcia,
>Elijah Aron, Jordan Young

AUGUST 31

Dying is a very dull, dreary affair. And my advice to you is to have nothing whatever to do with it.

W. Somerset Maugham
(1874 - 1965)

It is by universal misunderstanding that all agree. For if, by ill luck, people understood each other, they would never agree.

Charles Baudelaire (1821 - 1867)

Faith may be defined briefly as an illogical belief in the occurrence of the improbable.

H. L. Mencken (1880 - 1956)

Things are more like they are now than they have ever been.

Gerald R. Ford (1913 - 2006)

SEPTEMBER 1

Advice is what we ask for when we already know the answer but wish we didn't.

> Erica Jong

Tip the world over on its side and everything loose will land in Los Angeles.

> Frank Lloyd Wright
> (1869 - 1959)

If you're choking in a restaurant you can just say the magic words, 'Heimlich maneuver,' and all will be well. Trouble is, it's difficult to say 'Heimlich maneuver' when you're choking to death.

> Eddie Izzard

Rules are just helpful guidelines for stupid people who can't make up their own minds.

> Seth Hoffman

SEPTEMBER 2

I always keep a supply of stimulant handy in case I see a snake--which I also keep handy.

> W. C. Fields (1880 - 1946)

If at first you don't succeed, failure may be your style.

> Quentin Crisp

The greatest use of life is to spend it for something that will outlast it.

> William James (1842 - 1910)

There are no whole truths; all truths are half- truths. It is trying to treat them as whole truths that plays the devil.

> Alfred North Whitehead
> (1861 - 1947)

SEPTEMBER 3

Every journalist has a novel in him, which is an excellent place for it.

> Russel Lynes

The only thing that saves us from the bureaucracy is inefficiency. An efficient bureaucracy is the greatest threat to liberty.

> Eugene McCarthy (1916 - 2005)

There is an evil tendency underlying all our technology - the tendency to do what is reasonable even when it isn't any good.

> Robert Pirsig

I love being a writer. What I can't stand is the paperwork.

> Peter De Vries

SEPTEMBER 4

Things change when you hit the big 1-O. Your legs start to go, candy doesn't taste as good anymore.

>Bart Simpson

I have an existential map. It has 'You are here' written all over it.

>Steven Wright (1955 -)

I'm trying to be a sensitive father, you unwanted moron!

>Homer Simpson

Democracy consists of choosing your dictators, after they've told you what you think it is you want to hear.

>Alan Corenk

SEPTEMBER 5

A musicologist is a man who can read music but can't hear it.

> Sir Thomas Beecham
> (1879 - 1961)

A little more moderation would be good. Of course, my life hasn't exactly been one of moderation.

> Donald Trump (1946 -)

By the time I'd grown up, I naturally supposed that I'd be grown up.

> Eve Babitz

Never fight an inanimate object.
> P. J. O'Rourke (1947 -)

SEPTEMBER 6

Even if you're on the right track, you'll get run over if you just sit there.
> Will Rogers (1879 - 1935)

Patriotism is the willingness to kill and be killed for trivial reasons.
> Bertrand Russell (1872 - 1970)

The best way to keep children home is to make the home atmosphere pleasant--and let the air out of the tires.
> Dorothy Parker (1893 - 1967)

Whoso would be a man must be a nonconformist.
> Ralph Waldo Emerson (1803 - 1882)

SEPTEMBER 7

Underneath this flabby exterior is an enormous lack of character.

> Oscar Levant (1906 - 1972)

I despise the pleasure of pleasing people that I despise.

> Lady Mary Wortley Montagu
> (1689 - 1762)

Someday I want to be rich. Some people get so rich they lose all respect for humanity. That's how rich I want to be.

> Rita Rudner

Believe those who are seeking the truth. Doubt those who find it.

> Andre Gide (1869 - 1951)

SEPTEMBER 8

First secure an independent income, then practice virtue.

> Greek Proverb

Traditions are group efforts to keep the unexpected from happening.

> Barbara Tober

It has been my experience that folks who have no vices have very few virtues.

> Abraham Lincoln
> (1809 - 1865)

A perpetual holiday is a good working definition of hell.

> George Bernard Shaw
> (1856 - 1950)

SEPTEMBER 9

An honest politician is one who, when he is bought, will stay bought.

> Simon Cameron (1799 - 1889)

A lie can travel halfway around the world while the truth is putting on its shoes.

> Mark Twain (1835 - 1910)

Too many of us look upon Americans as dollar chasers. This is a cruel libel, even if it is reiterated thoughtlessly by the Americans themselves.

> Albert Einstein (1879 - 1955)

Those who agree with us may not be right, but we admire their astuteness.

> Cullen Hightower

SEPTEMBER 10

Television enables you to be entertained in your home by people you wouldn't have in your home.

>> David Frost

God is a comedian playing to an audience too afraid to laugh.

>> Voltaire (1694 - 1778)

When the politicians complain that TV turns the proceedings into a circus, it should be made clear that the circus was already there, and that TV has merely demonstrated that not all the performers are well trained.

>> Edward R. Murrow
>> (1908 - 1965)

A marriage is always made up of two people who are prepared to swear that only the other one snores.

>> Terry Pratchett

SEPTEMBER 11

I have discovered that all human evil comes from this, man's being unable to sit still in a room.

> Blaise Pascal (1623 - 1662)

I don't mind if you pee in the shower, but only if you're taking a shower.

> Marge Simpson

To err is human; to forgive, infrequent.

> Franklin P. Adams (1881 - 1960)

If time flies when you're having fun, it hits the afterburners when you don't think you're having enough.

> Jef Mallett

SEPTEMBER 12

A person is always startled when he hears himself seriously called an old man for the first time.

> Oliver Wendell Holmes
> (1809 - 1894)

Fervor is the weapon of choice for the impotent.

> Frantz Fanon

Ability will never catch up with the demand for it.

> Malcolm Forbes (1919 - 1990)

A committee can make a decision that is dumber than any of its members.

> David Coblitz

SEPTEMBER 13

Art is making something out of nothing and selling it.

> Frank Zappa (1940 - 1993)

It is not necessary to understand things in order to argue about them.

> Pierre Beaumarchais
> (1732 - 1799)

Everything you can imagine is real.

> Pablo Picasso (1881 - 1973)

I generally avoid temptation unless I can't resist it.

> Mae West (1892 - 1980)

SEPTEMBER 14

He played the king as if afraid someone else would play the ace.

>John Mason Brown (1900 - 1969)

I have suffered a great deal from writers who have quoted this or that sentence of mine either out of its context or in juxtaposition to some incongruous matter which quite distorted my meaning , or destroyed it altogether.

>Alfred North Whitehead
>(1861 - 1947)

Sometimes I get the feeling the whole world is against me, but deep down I know that's not true. Some smaller countries are neutral.

>Robert Orben

There's no justice like angry-mob justice.

>Seymour Skinner

SEPTEMBER 15

There is no reason for any individual to have a computer in his home.

> Ken Olsen (1926 -)

If we were not all so interested in ourselves, life would be so uninteresting that none of us would be able to endure it.

> Arthur Schopenhauer
> (1788 - 1860)

There are only two kinds of scholars; those who love ideas and those who hate them.

> Emile Chartier

A man can sleep around, no questions asked, but if a woman makes nineteen or twenty mistakes she's a tramp.

> Joan Rivers (1935 -)

SEPTEMBER 16

The best measure of a man's honesty isn't his income tax return. It's the zero adjust on his bathroom scale.

>Arthur C. Clarke (1917 -)

Misogynist: A man who hates women as much as women hate one another.

>H. L. Mencken (1880 - 1956)

Men who are unhappy, like men who sleep badly, are always proud of the fact.

>Bertrand Russell (1872 - 1970)

By a curious confusion, many modern critics have passed from the proposition that a masterpiece may be unpopular to the other proposition that unless it is unpopular it cannot be a masterpiece.

>G. K. Chesterton (1874 - 1936)

SEPTEMBER 17

If two men agree on everything, you may be sure that one of them is doing the thinking.

> Lyndon B. Johnson
> (1908 - 1973)

All paid jobs absorb and degrade the mind.

> Aristotle (384 BC - 322 BC)

Always get married early in the morning. That way, if it doesn't work out, you haven't wasted a whole day.

> Mickey Rooney (1920 -)

I passionately hate the idea of being with it, I think an artist has always to be out of step with his time.

> Orson Welles (1915 - 1985)

SEPTEMBER 18

Nothing is impossible. Some things are just less likely than others.

> Jonathan Winters

A lot of people like snow. I find it to be an unnecessary freezing of water.

> Carl Reiner

The artist doesn't have time to listen to the critics. The ones who want to be writers read the reviews, the ones who want to write don't have the time to read reviews.

> William Faulkner (1897 - 1962)

Damn it, Smithers! This isn't rocket science, it's brain surgery!

> Montgomery Burns

SEPTEMBER 19

A diplomat... is a person who can tell you to go to hell in such a way that you actually look forward to the trip.

Caskie Stinnett

Nobody in the game of football should be called a genius. A genius is somebody like Norman Einstein.

Joe Theismann

Making duplicate copies and computer printouts of things no one wanted even one of in the first place is giving America a new sense of purpose.

Andy Rooney (1919 -)

The people I distrust most are those who want to improve our lives but have only one course of action.

Frank Herbert (1920 - 1986)

SEPTEMBER 20

Biography lends to death a new terror.
> Oscar Wilde (1854 - 1900)

The great thing about television is that if something important happens anywhere in the world, day or night, you can always change the channel.
> From "Taxi"

The real art of conversation is not only to say the right thing at the right place but to leave unsaid the wrong thing at the tempting moment.
> Dorothy Nevill

There are only two ways of telling the complete truth--anonymously and posthumously.
> Thomas Sowell (1930 -)

SEPTEMBER 21

In this business you either sink or swim or you don't.

>David Smith

We are so vain that we even care for the opinion of those we don't care for.

>Marie Ebner von Eschenbach

We seem to believe it is possible to ward off death by following rules of good grooming.

>Don Delillo

There's so much comedy on television. Does that cause comedy in the streets?

>Dick Cavett (1936 -)

SEPTEMBER 22

The power of accurate observation is commonly called cynicism by those who have not got it.

> George Bernard Shaw
> (1856 - 1950)

I hate the outdoors. To me the outdoors is where the car is.

> Will Durst

Damn it, Smithers! This isn't rocket science, it's brain surgery!

> Montgomery Burns

A poem is never finished, only abandoned.

> Paul Valery (1871 - 1945)

SEPTEMBER 23

Horse sense is the thing a horse has which keeps it from betting on people.

                W. C. Fields (1880 - 1946)

Newspapermen learn to call a murderer 'an alleged murderer' and the King of England 'the alleged King of England' to avoid libel suits.

                Stephen Leacock (1869 - 1944)

My religion consists of a humble admiration of the illimitable superior spirit who reveals himself in the slight details we are able to perceive with our frail and feeble mind.

                Albert Einstein (1879 - 1955)

Whatever women do they must do twice as well as men to be thought half as good. Luckily this is not difficult.

                Charlotte Whitton

SEPTEMBER 24

Under capitalism, man exploits man. Under communism, it's just the opposite.

> John Kenneth Galbraith
> (1908 - 2006)

An epigram often flashes light into regions where reason shines but dimly.

> Edwin P. Whipple

If you hate a person, you hate something in him that is part of yourself. What isn't part of ourselves doesn't disturb us.

> Hermann Hesse (1877 - 1962)

Money can't buy happiness, but neither can poverty.

> Leo Rosten (1908 -)

SEPTEMBER 25

Never confuse movement with action.
> Ernest Hemingway
> (1899 - 1961)

A facility for quotation covers the absence of original thought.
> Dorothy L. Sayers (1893 - 1957)

Before I got married I had six theories about bringing up children; now I have six children and no theories.
> John Wilmot

If you don't know where you are going, any road will take you there.
> Lewis Carroll (1832 - 1898)

SEPTEMBER 26

I never lecture, not because I am shy or a bad speaker, but simply because I detest the sort of people who go to lectures and don't want to meet them.

> H. L. Mencken (1880 - 1956)

Works of art, in my opinion, are the only objects in the material universe to possess internal order, and that is why, though I don't believe that only art matters, I do believe in Art for Art's sake.

> E. M. Forster (1879 - 1970)

There's no secret about success. Did you ever know a successful man who didn't tell you about it?

> Kin Hubbard (1868 - 1930)

There art two cardinal sins from which all others spring: Impatience and Laziness.

> Franz Kafka (1883 - 1924)

SEPTEMBER 27

My toughest fight was with my first wife.

> Muhammad Ali (1942 -)

I find television very educating. Every time somebody turns on the set, I go into the other room and read a book.

> Groucho Marx (1890 - 1977)

He is one of those people who would be enormously improved by death.

> Saki (1870 - 1916)

Humility is the embarrassment you feel when you tell people how wonderful you are.

> Laurence J. Peter (1919 - 1988)

SEPTEMBER 28

It is a curious thing... that every creed promises a paradise which will be absolutely uninhabitable for anyone of civilized taste.

> Evelyn Waugh (1903 - 1966)

Nothing takes the taste out of peanut butter quite like unrequited love.

> Charles M. Schulz (1922 - 2000)

Every composer knows the anguish and despair occasioned by forgetting ideas which one had no time to write down.

> Hector Berlioz (1803 - 1869)

I hope that when I die, people say about me, 'Boy, that guy sure owed me a lot of money.'

> Jack Handey (1949 -)

SEPTEMBER 29

Competence, like truth, beauty and contact lenses, is in the eye of the beholder.

> Laurence J. Peter (1919 - 1988)

The reason lightning doesn't strike twice in the same place is that the same place isn't there the second time.

> Willie Tyler

He felt that his whole life was some kind of dream and he sometimes wondered whose it was and whether they were enjoying it.

> Douglas Adams (1952 - 2001)

No man remains quite what he was when he recognizes himself.

> Thomas Mann (1875 - 1955)

SEPTEMBER 30

Familiarity breeds contempt - and children.

> Mark Twain (1835 - 1910),
> Notebooks (1935)

It is true that I was born in Iowa, but I can't speak for my twin sister.

> Abigail Van Buren (1918 -),
> (Dear Abby)

A satirist is a man who discovers unpleasant things about himself and then says them about other people.

> Peter McArthur

If you develop an ear for sounds that are musical it is like developing an ego. You begin to refuse sounds that are not musical and that way cut yourself off from a good deal of experience.

> John Cage (1912 - 1992)

OCTOBER 1

When ideas fail, words come in very handy.

> Johann Wolfgang von Goethe
> (1749 - 1832)

In our civilization, and under our republican form of government, intelligence is so highly honored that it is rewarded by exemption from the cares of office.

> Ambrose Bierce (1842 - 1914)

That's the trouble with a politician's life-somebody is always interrupting it with an election.

> Will Rogers (1879 - 1935)

Nothing is more characteristic of a man than the manner in which he behaves toward fools.

> Henri-Frédéric Amiel

OCTOBER 2

Discovery consists of seeing what everybody has seen and thinking what nobody has thought.

> Albert Szent-Gyorgyi
> (1893 - 1986)

The trouble with jogging is that the ice falls out of your glass.

> Martin Mull (1943 -)

Most men pursue pleasure with such breathless haste that they hurry past it.

> Soren Kierkegaard
> (1813 - 1855)

The good life, as I conceive it, is a happy life. I do not mean that if you are good you will be happy - I mean that if you are happy you will be good.

> Bertrand Russell
> (1872 - 1970)

OCTOBER 3

There are two kinds of people, those who finish what they start and so on.

> Robert Byrne

He who can, does. He who cannot, teaches.

> George Bernard Shaw
> (1856 - 1950)

Against stupidity the gods themselves contend in vain.

> Friedrich von Schiller
> (1759 - 1805)

A man may be so much of everything that he is nothing of anything.

> Samuel Johnson (1709 - 1784)

OCTOBER 4

Any fool can tell the truth, but it requires a man of some sense to know how to lie well.

    Samuel Butler (1835 - 1902)

Quit worrying about your health. It'll go away.

    Robert Orben

This is Papa Bear. Put out an APB for a male suspect, driving a...car of some sort, heading in the direction of...you know, that place that sells chili. Suspect is hatless. Repeat, hatless.

    Clarence Wiggum

Under the greenwood tree who loves to lie with me ... Here shall he see no enemy but winter and rough weather.

    William Shakespeare
    (1564 - 1616)

OCTOBER 5

Welcome to Santa's Village, where it's Christmas everyday! Closed on Christmas.

> Simpsons Elf

Nothing is more conducive to peace of mind than not having any opinions at all.

> Georg Christoph Lichtenberg
> (1742 - 1799)

I love being married. It's so great to find that one special person you want to annoy for the rest of your life.

> Rita Rudner

Seek simplicity, and distrust it.

> Alfred North Whitehead
> (1861 - 1947)

OCTOBER 6

Part of the secret of success in life is to eat what you like and let the food fight it out inside.

> Mark Twain (1835 - 1910)

I have seen the future and it doesn't work.

> Robert Fulford

Let's go! If I'm not back at the home by nine they declare me legally dead and collect my insurance!

> Abraham Simpson

There's an old saying about those who forget history. I don't remember it, but it's good.

> Stephen Colbert

OCTOBER 7

Invention is the mother of necessity.
>Yogi Berra (1925 -)

Advertisements... contain the only truths to be relied on in a newspaper.
>Thomas Jefferson (1743 - 1826)

Ooh, I love your magazine. My favorite section is, "How To Increase Your Word Power." That thing is really, really...really...good.
>Homer Simpson

In modern America, anyone who attempts to write satirically about the events of the day finds it difficult to concoct a situation so bizarre that it may not actually come to pass while the article is still on the presses.
>Calvin Trillin (1935 -)

OCTOBER 8

A conservative is a man who believes that nothing should be done for the first time.

> Alfred E. Wiggam

We are the people our parents warned us about.

> Jimmy Buffett

No one can have a higher opinion of him than I have, and I think he's a dirty little beast.

> W. S. Gilbert (1836 - 1911)

It's not a matter of whether or not someone's watching over you. It's just a question of their intentions.

> Randy K. Milholland

OCTOBER 9

Reality is something you rise above.
>Liza Minnelli (1946 -)

A lawyer starts life giving $500 worth of law for $5 and ends giving $5 worth for $500.
>Benjamin H. Brewster
>(1816 - 1888)

The men who really believe in themselves are all in lunatic asylums.
>G. K. Chesterton (1874 - 1936)

Progress isn't made by early risers. It's made by lazy men trying to find easier ways to do something.
>Robert Heinlein (1907 - 1988)

OCTOBER 10

History is the short trudge from Adam to atom.

> Leonard Louis Levinson

The United States is a nation of laws: badly written and randomly enforced.

> Frank Zappa (1940 - 1993)

We need anything politically important rationed out like Pez: small, sweet, and coming out of a funny, plastic head.

> Dennis Miller

We can have facts without thinking but we cannot have thinking without facts.

> John Dewey (1859 - 1952)

OCTOBER 11

On my income tax 1040 it says 'Check this box if you are blind.' I wanted to put a check mark about three inches away.

> Tom Lehrer (1928 -)

Television has proved that people will look at anything rather than each other.

> Ann Landers (1918 - 2002)

My Homer is not a communist. He may be a liar, a pig, an idiot, a communist, but he is not a porn star.

> Abraham Simpson

That's the funny thing about havin' a kid. They come with their own set of problems; make everything else you were worried about seem kinda silly.

> Greg Garcia

OCTOBER 12

What's another word for Thesaurus?
> Steven Wright (1955 -)

The wit makes fun of other persons; the satirist makes fun of the world; the humorist makes fun of himself.
> James Thurber (1894 - 1961)

Sometimes what's right isn't as important as what's profitable.
> Trey Parker and Matt Stone

So this is how liberty dies. With thunderous applause.
> George Lucas (1944 -)

OCTOBER 13

I hate quotations. Tell me what you know.

> Ralph Waldo Emerson
> (1803 - 1882)

Nobody can be exactly like me. Sometimes even I have trouble doing it.

> Tallulah Bankhead (1903 - 1968)

Here's something to think about: How come you never see a headline like 'Psychic Wins Lottery'?

> Jay Leno (1950 -)

I always find it more difficult to say the things I mean than the things I don't.

> W. Somerset Maugham
> (1874 - 1965)

OCTOBER 14

A liberal is a man too broadminded to take his own side in a quarrel.

> Robert Frost (1874 - 1963)

He who hesitates is not only lost, but miles from the next exit.

> Unknown

I like to believe that people in the long run are going to do more to promote peace than our governments. Indeed, I think that people want peace so much that one of these days governments had better get out of the way and let them have it.

> Dwight D. Eisenhower
> (1890 - 1969)

Talent hits a target no one else can hit; Genius hits a target no one else can see.

> Arthur Schopenhauer
> (1788 - 1860)

OCTOBER 15

The cost of living is going up and the chance of living is going down.
>Flip Wilson (1933 - 1998)

I was born not knowing and have had only a little time to change that here and there.
>Richard Feynman (1918 - 1988)

Speak the truth, but leave immediately after.
>Slovenian Proverb

To be poor and dependent is very nearly an impossibility.
>William Cobbett (1763 - 1835)

OCTOBER 16

The best defense against the atom bomb is not to be there when it goes off.

> Anonymous

Genius may have its limitations, but stupidity is not thus handicapped.

> Elbert Hubbard (1856 - 1915)

I'm just trying to make a smudge on the collective unconscious.

> David Letterman (1947 -)

The secret of being a bore is to tell everything.

> Voltaire (1694 - 1778)

OCTOBER 17

Committee--a group of men who individually can do nothing but as a group decide that nothing can be done.

> Fred Allen (1894 - 1956)

He who asks is a fool for five minutes, but he who does not ask remains a fool forever.

> Chinese Proverb

I am determined that my children shall be brought up in their father's religion, if they can find out what it is.

> Charles Lamb (1775 - 1834)

I never met anybody who said when they were a kid, "I wanna grow up and be a critic."

> Richard Pryor (1940 - 2005)

OCTOBER 18

The secret of success is sincerity. Once you can fake that you've got it made.

> Jean Giraudoux (1882 - 1944)

Honesty pays, but it doesn't seem to pay enough to suit some people.

> Kin Hubbard (1868 - 1930)

A man is rich in proportion to the number of things he can afford to let alone.

> Henry David Thoreau
> (1817 - 1862)

Do you realize if it weren't for Edison we'd be watching TV by candlelight?

> Al Boliska

OCTOBER 19

The worst thing about Europe is that you can't go out in the middle of the night and get a Slurpee.

Tellis Frank

The nice thing about standards is that there are so many of them to choose from.

Andrew S. Tanenbaum

In the United States, doing good has come to be, like patriotism, a favorite device of persons with something to sell.

H. L. Mencken (1880 - 1956)

The keenest sorrow is to recognize ourselves as the sole cause of all our adversities.

Sophocles (496 BC - 406 BC)

OCTOBER 20

I believe that every human has a finite number of heart-beats. I don't intend to waste any of mine running around doing exercises.

Buzz Aldrin (1930 -)

A psychiatrist is a fellow who asks you a lot of expensive questions your wife asks for nothing.

Joey Adams

Television has done much for psychiatry by spreading information about it, as well as contributing to the need for it.

Alfred Hitchcock (1899 - 1980)

The world tolerates conceit from those who are successful, but not from anybody else.

John Blake

OCTOBER 21

Only sick music makes money today.

> Friedrich Nietzsche
> (1844 - 1900)

A lie told often enough becomes the truth.

> Lenin (1870 - 1924)

Any man whose errors take ten years to correct is quite a man.

> J. Robert Oppenheimer
> (1904 - 1967)

Literature is an occupation in which you have to keep proving your talent to people who have none.

> Jules Renard (1864 - 1910)

OCTOBER 22

In Paris they simply stared when I spoke to them in French; I never did succeed in making those idiots understand their language.

>Mark Twain (1835 - 1910)

Girls are always running through my mind. They don't dare walk.

>Andy Gibb

The only thing wrong with immortality is that it tends to go on forever.

>Herb Caen

I'll be more enthusiastic about encouraging thinking outside the box when there's evidence of any thinking going on inside it.

>Terry Pratchett

OCTOBER 23

In answer to the question of why it happened, I offer the modest proposal that our Universe is simply one of those things which happen from time to time.

> Edward P. Tryon

It is a sign of a creeping inner death when we no longer can praise the living.

> Eric Hoffer (1902 - 1983)

Beer. Now there's a temporary solution.

> Homer Simpson

If life was fair, Elvis would be alive and all the impersonators would be dead.

> Johnny Carson (1925 - 2005)

OCTOBER 24

A citizen of America will cross the ocean to fight for democracy, but won't cross the street to vote in a national election.

>Bill Vaughan

Art is either plagiarism or revolution.
>Paul Gauguin (1848 - 1903)

Dance like it hurts, Love like you need money, Work when people are watching.
>Scott Adams (1957 -)

Whenever two people meet, there are really six people present. There is each man as he sees himself, each man as the other person sees him, and each man as he really is.
>William James (1842 - 1910)

OCTOBER 25

They may say she died from a burst ventricle, but I know she died of a broken heart.

> Abraham Simpson

The only winner in the War of 1812 was Tchaikovsky.

> Solomon Short

The trouble with America is that there are far too many wide-open spaces surrounded by teeth.

> Charles Luckman

When we ask for advice, we are usually looking for an accomplice.

> Marquis de la Grange
> (1639 - 1692)

OCTOBER 26

If it turns out that there is a God, I don't think that he's evil. But the worst that you can say about him is that basically he's an underachiever.

> Woody Allen (1935 -)

Science has proof without any certainty. Creationists have certainty without any proof.

> Ashley Montague

Education is a state-controlled manufactory of echoes.

> Norman Douglas

It is unbecoming for young men to utter maxims.

> Aristotle (384 BC - 322 BC)

OCTOBER 27

I think that I shall never see a billboard lovely as a tree. Perhaps, unless the billboards fall, I'll never see a tree at all.

>Ogden Nash (1902 - 1971)

Actions lie louder than words.

>Carolyn Wells

Special-interest publications should realize that if they are attracting enough advertising and readers to make a profit, the interest is not so special.

>Fran Lebowitz (1950 -)

If he was going to commit a crime, would he have invited the number one cop in town? Now where did I put my gun? Oh yeah, I set it down when I got a piece of cake.

>Clarence Wiggum

OCTOBER 28

For every person who wants to teach there are approximately thirty people who don't want to learn--much.

> W. C. Sellar
> and R. J. Yeatman

Why be a man when you can be a success?

> Bertolt Brecht (1898 - 1956)

Acting is not being emotional, but being able to express emotion.

> Kate Reid

Love is an exploding cigar we willingly smoke.

> Lynda Barry

OCTOBER 29

The world is full of willing people, some willing to work, the rest willing to let them.

>Robert Frost (1874 - 1963)

I think we'd be all better off if each country had its own planet.

>Barney Gumble

Human history becomes more and more a race between education and catastrophe.

>H. G. Wells (1866 - 1946)

Well, the telling of jokes is an art of its own, and it always rises from some emotional threat. The best jokes are dangerous, and dangerous because they are in some way truthful.

>Kurt Vonnegut (1922 - 2007)

OCTOBER 30

Don't use a big word where a diminutive one will suffice.

> Unknown

There's always somebody who is paid too much, and taxed too little - and it's always somebody else.

> Cullen Hightower

I work from midnight to eight, come home, sleep for five minutes, eat breakfast, sleep six more minutes, shower, then I have ten minutes to bask in Lisa's love, then I'm off to the power plant, fresh as a daisy.

> Homer Simpson

Exercise relieves stress. Nothing relieves exercise.

> Takayuki Ikkaku, Arisa Hosaka and Toshihiro Kawabata

OCTOBER 31

If you drink, don't drive. Don't even putt.

> Dean Martin

Everything is in a state of flux, including the status quo.

> Robert Byrne

Ancient Rome declined because it had a Senate; now what's going to happen to us with both a Senate and a House?

> Will Rogers (1879 - 1935)

I became a feminist as an alternative to becoming a masochist.

> Sally Kempton

NOVEMBER 1

The world is round; it has no point.
> Adrienne E. Gusoff

From now on our family is eating healthy food that looks bad on the shelf and good in our colon.
> Marge Simpson

Discretion is not the better part of biography.
> Lytton Strachey (1880 - 1932)

In the part of this universe that we know there is great injustice, and often the good suffer, and often the wicked prosper, and one hardly knows which of those is the more annoying.
> Bertrand Russell (1872 - 1970)

NOVEMBER 2

The mystery of government is not how Washington works but how to make it stop.

> P. J. O'Rourke (1947 -)

Human beings are the only creatures that allow their children to come back home.

> Bill Cosby (1937 -)

There is nothing new under the sun but there are lots of old things we don't know.

> Ambrose Bierce (1842 - 1914)

It is not bigotry to be certain we are right; but it is bigotry to be unable to imagine how we might possibly have gone wrong.

> G. K. Chesterton (1874 - 1936)

NOVEMBER 3

We learn something every day, and lots of times it's that what we learned the day before was wrong.

                          Bill Vaughan

The surest way to make a monkey of a man is to quote him.

                Robert Benchley (1889 - 1945)

Against logic there is no armor like ignorance.

                Laurence J. Peter (1919 - 1988)

If a man will begin with certainties, he shall end in doubts; but if he will be content to begin with doubts he shall end in certainties.

               Sir Francis Bacon (1561 - 1626)

NOVEMBER 4

Life is a foreign language; all men mispronounce it.

> Christopher Morley
> (1890 - 1957)

The only sure thing about luck is that it will change.

> Bret Harte (1836 - 1902)

Always be wary of any helpful item that weighs less than its operating manual.

> Terry Pratchett

A dime? What do you think I am, a payphone from 1980?

> Lisa Simpson

NOVEMBER 5

A national debt, if it is not excessive, will be to us a national blessing.

> Alexander Hamilton
> (1755 - 1804)

Instant gratification takes too long.
> Carrie Fisher (1956 -)

Philosophy is a battle against the bewitchment of our intelligence by means of language.

> Ludwig Wittgenstein
> (1889 - 1951)

Slap a mask on a drunk and you're going to have trouble. It's like having a live reenactment of anonymous forum comments.

> Randy K. Milholland

NOVEMBER 6

A wise man will make more opportunities than he finds.

>Sir Francis Bacon (1561 - 1626)

Why is it that our memory is good enough to retain the least triviality that happens to us, and yet not good enough to recollect how often we have told it to the same person?

>Francois de La Rochefoucauld
>(1613 - 1680)

The more things a man is ashamed of, the more respectable he is.

>George Bernard Shaw
>(1856 - 1950)

Morality, like art, means drawing a line someplace.

>Oscar Wilde (1854 - 1900)

NOVEMBER 7

The entire economy of the Western world is built on things that cause cancer.

> From the 1985 movie "Bliss"

Happy families are all alike; every unhappy family is unhappy in its own way.

> Leo Tolstoy (1828 - 1910)

Charm is the quality in others that makes us more satisfied with ourselves.

> Henri-Frédéric Amiel

I know who I am. No one else knows who I am. If I was a giraffe, and someone said I was a snake, I'd think, no, actually I'm a giraffe.

> Richard Gere

NOVEMBER 8

Ninety-eight percent of the adults in this country are decent, hard-working, honest Americans. It's the other lousy two percent that get all the publicity. But then--we elected them.

>Lily Tomlin (1939 -)

The ultimate result of shielding men from the effects of folly is to fill the world with fools.

>Herbert Spencer (1820 - 1903)

Kill myself? Killing myself is the last thing I'd ever do. Now I have a purpose, a reason to live. I don't care who I have to face. I don't care who I have to fight. I will not rest until this street gets a stop sign!

>Homer Simpson

In journalism, there has always been a tension between getting it first and getting it right.

>Ellen Goodman (1941 -)

NOVEMBER 9

I don't deserve this award, but I have arthritis and I don't deserve that either.

> Jack Benny (1894 - 1974)

I do not take a single newspaper, nor read one a month, and I feel myself infinitely the happier for it.

> Thomas Jefferson
> (1743 - 1826)

You cannot depend on your eyes when your imagination is out of focus.

> Mark Twain (1835 - 1910)

Laughing at our mistakes can lengthen our own life. Laughing at someone else's can shorten it.

> Cullen Hightower

NOVEMBER 10

Politics is the art of preventing people from taking part in affairs which properly concern them.

>Paul Valery (1871 - 1945)

Imagination is more important than knowledge...

>Albert Einstein (1879 - 1955)

Cockroaches and socialites are the only things that can stay up all night and eat anything.

>Herb Caen

After being Turned Down by numerous Publishers, he had decided to write for Posterity.

>George Ade (1866 - 1944)

NOVEMBER 11

Acting is merely the art of keeping a large group of people from coughing.

> Sir Ralph Richardson
> (1902 - 1983)

Technology is dominated by two types of people: those who understand what they do not manage, and those who manage what they do not understand.

> Putt's Law

There is no moral precept that does not have something inconvenient about it.

> Denis Diderot (1713 - 1784)

Being a woman is a terribly difficult task since it consists principally in dealing with men.

> Joseph Conrad (1857 - 1924)

NOVEMBER 12

Research is the process of going up alleys to see if they are blind.

> Marston Bates

Rogues are preferable to imbeciles because they sometimes take a rest.

> Alexandre Dumas (1802 - 1870)

Happiness is not achieved by the conscious pursuit of happiness; it is generally the by-product of other activities.

> Aldous Huxley (1894 - 1963)

O, what may man within him hide, though angel on the outward side!

> William Shakespeare
> (1564 - 1616)

NOVEMBER 13

I envy people who drink. At least they have something to blame everything on.

>Oscar Levant (1906 - 1972)

Thought is only a flash between two long nights, but this flash is everything.

>Henri Poincare (1854 - 1912)

We live in a Newtonian world of Einsteinian physics ruled by Frankenstein logic.

>David Russell

Whenever you hear the consensus of scientists agrees on something or other, reach for your wallet, because you're being had.

>Michael Crichton (1942 - 2008)

NOVEMBER 14

A man with a watch knows what time it is. A man with two watches is never sure.

> Segal's Law

When I read about the evils of drinking, I gave up reading.

> Henny Youngman
> (1906 - 1998)

I do not have a psychiatrist and I do not want one, for the simple reason that if he listened to me long enough, he might become disturbed.

> James Thurber (1894 - 1961)

In America, through pressure of conformity, there is freedom of choice, but nothing to choose from.

> Peter Ustinov (1921 - 2004)

NOVEMBER 15

Wagner's music is better than it sounds.

> Edgar Wilson Nye
> (1850 - 1896)

Old age is not so bad when you consider the alternatives.

> Maurice Chevalier
> (1888 - 1972)

Smoking is one of the leading causes of statistics.

> Fletcher Knebel

Television – a medium. So called because it is neither rare nor well done.

> Ernie Kovacs

NOVEMBER 16

A single death is a tragedy; a million deaths is a statistic.

> Joseph Stalin (1879 - 1953)

Few things are more satisfying than seeing your own children have teenagers of their own.

> Doug Larson

Old age is the most unexpected of all the things that happen to a man.

> Leon Trotsky (1879 - 1940)

Here's a tip to avoid death by celebrity: First off, get a life. They can't touch you if you're out doing something interesting.

> Kent Nichols
> and Douglas Sarine

NOVEMBER 17

Every improvement in communication makes the bore more terrible.
> Frank Moore Colby

Aren't we forgetting the true meaning of Christmas: the birth of Santa?
> Bart Simpson

Leave it to a girl to take the fun out of sex discrimination.
> Bill Watterson (1958 -)

If you are a dog and your owner suggests that you wear a sweater, suggest that he wear a tail.
> Fran Lebowitz (1950 -)

NOVEMBER 18

If God lived on earth, people would break his windows.

> Jewish Proverb

Any fool can criticize, condemn, and complain - and most fools do.

> Dale Carnegie

Television has raised writing to a new low.

> Samuel Goldwyn (1882 - 1974)

A sense of duty is useful in work, but offensive in personal relations. People wish to be liked, not be endured with patient resignation.

> Bertrand Russell (1872 - 1970)

NOVEMBER 19

I suppose that I shall have to die beyond my means.

                Oscar Wilde (1854 - 1900)

What a pity, when Christopher Colombus discovered America, that he ever mentioned it.

                Margot Asquith

Man is tormented by no greater anxiety than to find someone quickly to whom he can hand over that great gift of freedom with which the ill-fated creature is born.

                Fyodor Dostoevsky
                (1821 - 1881)

Maybe I should just cut my losses, give up on Lisa, and make a fresh start with Maggie.

                Homer Simpson

NOVEMBER 20

Yes, I've kissed a lot of guys. I like to kiss, but that's it. I don't go home with anyone. I sleep with my animals, like my baby monkey, Brigitte Bardot.

>Paris Hilton

If you are not criticized, you may not be doing much.

>Donald H. Rumsfeld (1932 -)

You're in the newspaper business? Something that's going to die before I do.

>Abraham Simpson

When a man comes to me for advice, I find out the kind of advice he wants, and I give it to him.

>John Billings
>(Henry Wheeler Shaw)

NOVEMBER 21

All of us learn to write in the second grade. Most of us go on to greater things.

> Bobby Knight (1940 -)

I know not, sir, whether Bacon wrote the works of Shakespeare, but if he did not it seems to me that he missed the opportunity of his life.

> James M. Barrie (1860 - 1937)

A writer is a person for whom writing is more difficult than it is for other people.

> Thomas Mann (1875 - 1955)

I like nonsense, it wakes up the brain cells. Fantasy is a necessary ingredient in living, It's a way of looking at life through the wrong end of a telescope. Which is what I do, And that enables you to laugh at life's realities.

> Dr. Seuss (1904 - 1991)

NOVEMBER 22

If it weren't for Philo T. Farnsworth, inventor of television, we'd still be eating frozen radio dinners.

>Johnny Carson (1925 - 2005)

Lack of money is no obstacle. Lack of an idea is an obstacle.

>Ken Hakuta

You know what's interesting about Washington? It's the kind of place where second-guessing has become second nature.

>George W. Bush (1946 -)

We don't bother much about dress and manners in England, because as a nation we don't dress well and we've no manners.

>George Bernard Shaw
>(1856 - 1950)

NOVEMBER 23

I was a vegetarian until I started leaning toward the sunlight.

> Rita Rudner

Fortune does not change men, it unmasks them.

> Suzanne Necker (1739 - 1794)

Whoa, slow down there maestro. There's a NEW Mexico?

> Montgomery Burns

Knowledge is power, if you know it about the right person.

> Ethel Mumford

NOVEMBER 24

After I'm dead I'd rather have people ask why I have no monument than why I have one.

> Cato the Elder
> (234 BC - 149 BC)

Foolish writers and readers are created for each other.

> Horace Walpole (1717 - 1797)

All truth passes through three stages. First, it is ridiculed. Second, it is violently opposed. Third, it is accepted as being self-evident.

> Arthur Schopenhauer
> (1788 - 1860)

Many would be cowards if they had courage enough.

> Thomas Fuller (1608 - 1661)

NOVEMBER 25

Talking out of turn...that's a paddling. Looking out the window...that's a paddling. Staring at my sandals...that's a paddling. Paddling the school canoe...ooh, you better believe that's a paddling.

> Jaspar Beardly

Youth would be an ideal state if it came a little later in life.

> Herbert Henry Asquith
> (1852 - 1928)

A fanatic is one who can't change his mind and won't change the subject.

> Sir Winston Churchill
> (1874 - 1965)

There is no stigma attached to recognizing a bad decision in time to install a better one.

> Laurence J. Peter
> (1919 - 1988)

NOVEMBER 26

The folly of mistaking a paradox for a discovery, a metaphor for a proof, a torrent of verbiage for a spring of capital truths, and oneself for an oracle, is inborn in us.

> Paul Valery (1871 - 1945)

Take everything you like seriously, except yourselves.

> Rudyard Kipling (1865 - 1936)

Statistician: A man who believes figures don't lie, but admits that under analysis some of them won't stand up either.

> Evan Esar (1899 - 1995)

Read, every day, something no one else is reading. Think, every day, something no one else is thinking. Do, every day, something no one else would be silly enough to do. It is bad for the mind to be always part of unanimity.

> Christopher Morley
> (1890 - 1957)

NOVEMBER 27

When a thing has been said and well, have no scruple. Take it and copy it.

>   Anatole France (1844 - 1924)

If you put tomfoolery into a computer, nothing comes out of it but tomfoolery. But this tomfoolery, having passed through a very expensive machine, is somehow ennobled and no-one dares criticize it.

>   Pierre Gallois

Love is the triumph of imagination over intelligence.

>   H. L. Mencken (1880 - 1956)

Devotees of grammatical studies have not been distinguished for any very remarkable felicities of expression.

>   Amos Bronson Alcott
>   (1799 - 1888)

NOVEMBER 28

A country can be judged by the quality of its proverbs.

> German Proverb

Facts are stupid things.
> Ronald Reagan (1911 - 2004)

Students achieving Oneness will move on to Twoness.

> Woody Allen (1935 -)

The goal of all inanimate objects is to resist man and ultimately defeat him.

> Russell Baker (1925 -)

NOVEMBER 29

Some people change when they think they're a star or something.

> Paris Hilton

Kids, just because I don't care doesn't mean I'm not listening.

> Homer Simpson

Everyone's a hero in their own way, in their own not that heroic way.

> Joss Whedon, Zack Whedon, Maurissa Tancharoen, and Jed Whedon

The world only goes round by misunderstanding.

> Charles Baudelaire (1821 - 1867)

NOVEMBER 30

When we remember we are all mad, the mysteries disappear and life stands explained.

> Mark Twain (1835 - 1910)

People who get nostalgic about childhood were obviously never children.

> Bill Watterson (1958 -)

Being in politics is like being a football coach. You have to be smart enough to understand the game, and dumb enough to think it's important.

> Eugene McCarthy
> (1916 - 2005)

What's done cannot be undone.

> William Shakespeare
> (1564 - 1616)

DECEMBER 1

Everyone is born with genius, but most people only keep it a few minutes.

>Edgard Varese (1883 - 1965)

Take care of the luxuries and the necessities will take care of themselves.

>Dorothy Parker (1893 - 1967)

Remember the time he ate my goldfish, and you lied to me and said I never had any goldfish. Then why'd I have the bowl, Bart? Why did I have the bowl?

>Milhouse Van Houten

In a time of universal deceit, telling the truth is a revolutionary act.

>George Orwell (1903 - 1950)

DECEMBER 2

I never forget a face, but in your case I'll be glad to make an exception.

> Groucho Marx (1890 - 1977)

All power corrupts, but we need the electricity.

> Unknown

A desk is a dangerous place from which to watch the world.

> John le Carre (1931 -)

He slept, he stole, he was rude to the customers. Still, there goes the best damned employee a convenience store ever had.

> Apu Nahasapeemapetilon

DECEMBER 3

We don't know a millionth of one percent about anything.

> Thomas A. Edison
> (1847 - 1931)

There is no such thing as a moral or an immoral book. Books are well written or badly written.

> Oscar Wilde (1854 - 1900)

One of the most obvious facts about grownups to a child is that they have forgotten what it is like to be a child.

> Randall Jarrell (1914 - 1965)

He may be mad, but there's method in his madness. There nearly always is method in madness. It's what drives men mad, being methodical.

> G. K. Chesterton (1874 - 1936)

DECEMBER 4

Anybody caught selling macrame in public should be dyed a natural color and hung out to dry.

> Calvin Trillin (1935 -)

It's a poor sort of memory that only works backward.

> Lewis Carroll (1832 - 1898)

It is our responsibilities, not ourselves, that we should take seriously.

> Peter Ustinov (1921 - 2004)

When I was a kid my parents moved a lot, but I always found them.

> Rodney Dangerfield
> (1921 - 2004)

DECEMBER 5

I am always doing that which I can not do, in order that I may learn how to do it.

> Pablo Picasso (1881 - 1973)

Another possible source of guidance for teenagers is television, but television's message has always been that the need for truth, wisdom and world peace pales by comparison with the need for a toothpaste that offers whiter teeth *and* fresher breath.

> Dave Barry (1947 -)

It was no wonder that people were so horrible when they started life as children.

> Kingsley Amis (1922 - 1995)

There are two things that will be believed of any man whatsoever, and one of them is that he has taken to drink.

> Booth Tarkington (1869 - 1946)

DECEMBER 6

When love is gone, there's always justice. And when justice is gone, there's always force. And when force is gone, there's always Mom. Hi, Mom!

> Laurie Anderson

To be stupid, selfish, and have good health are three requirements for happiness, though if stupidity is lacking, all is lost.

> Gustave Flaubert (1821 - 1880)

Knowledge is of two kinds. We know a subject ourselves, or we know where we can find information on it.

> Samuel Johnson (1709 - 1784)

If you live to be one hundred, you've got it made. Very few people die past that age.

> George Burns (1896 - 1996)

DECEMBER 7

What we become depends on what we read after all of the professors have finished with us. The greatest university of all is a collection of books.

>Thomas Carlyle (1795 - 1881)

In the United States there is more space where nobody is than where anybody is. That is what makes America what it is.

>Gertrude Stein (1874 - 1946)

The only rules comedy can tolerate are those of taste, and the only limitations those of libel.

>James Thurber (1894 - 1961)

The man of knowledge must be able not only to love his enemies but also to hate his friends.

>Friedrich Nietzsche (1844 - 1900)

DECEMBER 8

Joe's crematorium...you kill 'em, we grill 'em.

> Bart Simpson

I hate to advocate drugs, alcohol, violence, or insanity to anyone, but they've always worked for me.

> Hunter S. Thompson
> (1939 - 2005)

Health consists of having the same diseases as one's neighbors.

> Quentin Crisp

Bureaucracy defends the status quo long past the time when the quo has lost its status.

> Laurence J. Peter
> (1919 - 1988)

DECEMBER 9

Last night I dreamed I ate a ten-pound marshmallow, and when I woke up the pillow was gone.

> Tommy Cooper

A cynic is a man who, when he smells flowers, looks around for a coffin.

> H. L. Mencken (1880 - 1956)

The first time I see a jogger smiling, I'll consider it.

> Joan Rivers (1935 -)

Fine, we'll both go, and if anyone asks you something you don't understand, just say protons.

> Homer Simpson

DECEMBER 10

If all economists were laid end to end, they would not reach a conclusion.

> George Bernard Shaw
> (1856 - 1950)

Acting is the most minor of gifts and not a very high-class way to earn a living. After all, Shirley Temple could do it at the age of four.

> Katharine Hepburn
> (1907 - 2003)

Moral indignation is jealousy with a halo.

> H. G. Wells

'Whom are you?' he asked, for he had attended business college.

> George Ade (1866 - 1944)

DECEMBER 11

Try as hard as we may for perfection, the net result of our labors is an amazing variety of imperfectness. We are surprised at our own versatility in being able to fail in so many different ways.

> Samuel McChord Crothers

We always like those who admire us; we do not always like those whom we admire.

> Francois de La Rochefoucauld
> (1613 - 1680)

It was enough to make a body ashamed of the human race.

> Mark Twain (1835 - 1910)

The best ideas come as jokes. Make your thinking as funny as possible.

> David M. Ogilvy

DECEMBER 12

It's the good girls who keep diaries; the bad girls never have the time.

> Tallulah Bankhead
> (1903 - 1968)

There is no excellent beauty that hath not some strangeness in the proportion.

> Sir Francis Bacon
> (1561 - 1626)

Never go out to meet trouble. If you will just sit still, nine cases out of ten someone will intercept it before it reaches you.

> Calvin Coolidge
> (1872 - 1933)

That is the greatest fallacy, the wisdom of old men. They do not grow wise. They grow careful.

> Ernest Hemingway
> (1899 - 1961)

DECEMBER 13

Posterity is as likely to be wrong as anyone else.

> Heywood Broun
> (1888 - 1939)

It is far more impressive when others discover your good qualities without your help.

> Judith Martin

Most turkeys taste better the day after; my mother's tasted better the day before.

> Rita Rudner

About the time we think we can make ends meet, somebody moves the ends.

> Herbert Hoover
> (1874 - 1964)

DECEMBER 14

Brass bands are all very well in their place - outdoors and several miles away.

>Sir Thomas Beecham
>(1879 - 1961)

A good friend can tell you what is the matter with you in a minute. He may not seem such a good friend after telling.

>Arthur Brisbane

The greatest challenge to any thinker is stating the problem in a way that will allow a solution.

>Bertrand Russell
>(1872 - 1970)

The perfect bureaucrat everywhere is the man who manages to make no decisions and escape all responsibility.

>Brooks Atkinson
>(1894 - 1984)

DECEMBER 15

Examinations are formidable even to the best prepared, for the greatest fool may ask more than the wisest man can answer.

Charles Caleb Colton
(1780 - 1832)

I've been on a diet for two weeks and all I've lost is two weeks.

Totie Fields

Most advances in science come when a person for one reason or another is forced to change fields.

Peter Borden

Another flaw in the human character is that everybody wants to build and nobody wants to do maintenance.

Kurt Vonnegut (1922 - 2007)

DECEMBER 16

When a man tells you that he got rich through hard work, ask him: 'Whose?'
> Don Marquis (1878 - 1937)

If you aren't fired with enthusiasm, you will be fired with enthusiasm.
> Vince Lombardi (1913 - 1970)

The truth does not change according to our ability to stomach it.
> Flannery O'Connor
> (1925 - 1964)

Actually, I value every second we're together, from the moment I squeeze his orange juice in the morning till I tuck him in at night. He's not just my boss, he's my best friend too.
> Waylon Smithers, Jr.

DECEMBER 17

If God wanted us to fly, He would have given us tickets.

                      Mel Brooks (1926 -)

If there's anything unsettling to the stomach, it's watching actors on television talk about their personal lives.

                  Marlon Brando (1924 - 2004)

Indecision may or may not be my problem.

                        Jimmy Buffett

Every man is a damn fool for at least five minutes every day; wisdom consists of not exceeding the limit.

                Elbert Hubbard (1856 - 1915)

DECEMBER 18

Life is something that everyone should try at least once.

> Henry J. Tillman

If mankind minus one were of one opinion, then mankind is no more justified in silencing the one than the one - if he had the power - would be justified in silencing mankind.

> John Stuart Mill (1806 - 1873)

The trouble about trying to make yourself stupider than you really are is that you very often succeed.

> C. S. Lewis (1898 - 1963)

I'm a public servant, Seymour, I'm not allowed to use my own judgement in any way whatsoever.

> Gary Chalmers

DECEMBER 19

You've got the wrong number. This is 9-1... 2.

Clarence Wiggum

Correct me if I'm wrong, but hasn't the fine line between sanity and madness gotten finer?

George Price

The average man, who does not know what to do with his life, wants another one which will last forever.

Anatole France (1844 - 1924)

Careful. We don't want to learn from this.

Bill Watterson (1958 -)

DECEMBER 20

Usually, terrible things that are done with the excuse that progress requires them are not really progress at all, but just terrible things.

> Russell Baker (1925 -)

Autobiography is an unrivaled vehicle for telling the truth about other people.

> Philip Guedalla (1889 - 1944)

I prefer the company of peasants because they have not been educated sufficiently to reason incorrectly.

> Michel de Montaigne
> (1533 - 1592)

Indeed, history is nothing more than a tableau of crimes and misfortunes.

> Voltaire (1694 - 1778)

DECEMBER 21

Those who dream by day are cognizant of many things which escape those who dream only by night.

Edgar Allan Poe
(1809 - 1849)

'Who are you and how did you get in here?' 'I'm a locksmith. And, I'm a locksmith.'

Leslie Nielsen (1926 - 2010)

Humor is always based on a modicum of truth. Have you ever heard a joke about a father-in-law?

Dick Clark

Channeling is just bad ventriloquism. You use another voice, but people can see your lips moving.

Penn Jillette (1955 -)

DECEMBER 22

I've been called ugly, pug ugly, fugly, pug fugly, but never ugly ugly.

>Morris Szyslak

I can't bring myself to say, 'Well, I guess I'll be toddling along.' It isn't that I can't toddle. It's just that I can't guess I'll toddle.

>Robert Benchley (1889 - 1945)

Who'd have thought a nuclear reactor would be so complicated!

>Homer Simpson

School is learning things you don't want to know, surrounded by people you wish you didn't know, while working toward a future you don't know will ever come.

>Dave Kellett

DECEMBER 23

The fact that an opinion has been widely held is no evidence whatever that it is not utterly absurd; indeed in view of the silliness of the majority of mankind, a widespread belief is more likely to be foolish than sensible.

                Bertrand Russell (1872 - 1970)

Don't part with your illusions. When they are gone you may still exist, but you have ceased to live.

                     Mark Twain (1835 - 1910)

The main dangers in this life are the people who want to change everything - or nothing.

                    Nancy Astor (1879 - 1964)

If it were done, when 'tis done, then 'twere well it were done quickly.

                    William Shakespeare
                            (1564 - 1616)

DECEMBER 24

Life is a sexually transmitted disease.

> R. D. Laing

Humanity has advanced, when it has advanced, not because it has been sober, responsible, and cautious, but because it has been playful, rebellious, and immature.

> Tom Robbins (1936 -)

Life is an unbroken succession of false situations.

> Thornton Wilder (1897 - 1975)

In all large corporations, there is a pervasive fear that someone, somewhere is having fun with a computer on company time. Networks help alleviate that fear.

> John C. Dvorak

DECEMBER 25

Eternity's a terrible thought. I mean, where's it all going to end?

> Tom Stoppard (1937 -)

The reverse side also has a reverse side.

> Japanese Proverb

Equal opportunity means everyone will have a fair chance at being incompetent.

> Laurence J. Peter
> (1919 - 1988)

The more original a discovery, the more obvious it seems afterwards.

> Arthur Koestler
> (1905 - 1983)

DECEMBER 26

When a woman says nothing's wrong, that means everything's wrong. And when a woman says everything's wrong, that means everything's wrong. And when a woman says something's not funny, you'd better not laugh your ass off.

> Homer Simpson

When a man says he approves of something in principle, it means he hasn't the slightest intention of putting it into practice.

> Otto von Bismarck
> (1815 - 1898)

Never go to bed mad. Stay up and fight.

> Phyllis Diller

Think twice before you speak, and then you may be able to say something more insulting than if you spoke right out at once.

> Evan Esar (1899 - 1995)

DECEMBER 27

Every day, in every way, I am getting better and better.
> Emile Coue (1857 - 1926)

Man has to suffer. When he has no real afflictions, he invents some.
> Jose Marti

The opposite of the religious fanatic is not the fanatical atheist but the gentle cynic who cares not whether there is a god or not.
> Eric Hoffer (1902 - 1983)

I've always found paranoia to be a perfectly defensible position.
> Pat Conroy (1945 -)

DECEMBER 28

On the plus side, death is one of the few things that can be done just as easily lying down.

> Woody Allen (1935 -)

Hello, operator! Give me the number for 911!

> Homer Simpson

He's simply got the instinct for being unhappy highly developed.

> Saki (1870 - 1916)

To have doubted one's own first principles is the mark of a civilized man.

> Oliver Wendell Holmes Jr.
> (1841 - 1935)

DECEMBER 29

Fashion is something that goes in one year and out the other.

>Unknown

My pessimism extends to the point of even suspecting the sincerity of the pessimists.

>Jean Rostand (1894 - 1977)

Like its politicians and its wars, society has the teenagers it deserves.

>J. B. Priestley (1894 - 1984)

It is always easier to believe than to deny. Our minds are naturally affirmative.

>John Burroughs (1837 - 1921)

DECEMBER 30

At my lemonade stand I used to give the first glass away free and charge five dollars for the second glass. The refill contained the antidote.

> Emo Phillips

I have such poor vision I can date anybody.

> Garry Shandling (1949 -)

You must first have a lot of patience to learn to have patience.

> Stanislaw J. Lec
> (1909 - 1966)

When you're through changing, you're through.

> Bruce Barton

DECEMBER 31

Facts do not cease to exist because they are ignored.

> Aldous Huxley (1894 - 1963)

Oh, I'm in no condition to drive. Wait a minute. I don't have to listen to myself. I'm drunk.

> Homer Simpson

It has long been an axiom of mine that the little things are infinitely the most important.

> Sir Arthur Conan Doyle
> (1859 - 1930)

Beware of no man more than yourself; we carry our worst enemies within us.

> G. K. Chesterton
> (1874 - 1936)

AFTERWORD

I hope you were inspired by this year-long read to have success, laugh, and be motivated.

Putting this book together has been an enriching experience that I am privileged to share with you. Many of these quotes are now my familiar old friends.

Although we have technology to help us, we're all busy nowadays, and I hope that you can spare a few minutes each day to enrich your soul.

To a content purpose-driven life!

Much love,
Aaron Bartlett

If this book was helpful to you, please leave a review of it on Amazon! Each review you leave helps me write more books.

For the latest news on new quote books by Aaron Bartlett, please sign up for updates! It's easiest to keep you informed via email!

Sign up for updates by going to;
http://www.toppingspublishing.com/aaronbartlett

CPSIA information can be obtained
at www.ICGtesting.com
Printed in the USA
BVHW01s0116131217
502675BV00001BA/6/P